COLLECTING PICTURES

GUY R. WILLIAMS

Collecting Pictures

ARCO PUBLICATIONS

First published 1967 by Arco Publications

Copyright © Guy R. Williams 1967

Printed in Great Britain by

Ebenezer Baylis & Son Ltd

The Trinity Press

Worcester, and London

For
JOYCE PEYTON

'We ought to envy collectors,
for they brighten their days
with a long and peaceable joy.'
ANATOLE FRANCE

CONTENTS

1 Pictures for Pleasure   *Page* 13

2 How to Hang, Light and Store Pictures   25

3 A Good Picture Deserves a Good Frame   30

4 How to Build up a Collection of Pictures
   without going Bankrupt   42

5 Collecting Oil-paintings   53

6 Collecting Water-colours   64

7 Collecting Drawings   74

8 Collecting Relief and Intaglio Prints   86

9 Collecting Lithographs and Screen Prints   105

10 Collecting Sporting Pictures   114

11 Cleaning and Restoring   122

12 Fakes and Forgeries   128

13 Windfalls   138

Index   143

PLATES

P. J. Van Brussel: Flowerpiece   *Facing page* 32

R. G. Eves, r.a.: Leslie Howard   33

Richard Cosway, r.a.: Unfinished Miniature Portrait of Madame Du Barry   33

Clarkson Stanfield, r.a.: On the Dogger Bank   48

James Ward, r.a.: Bulls Fighting; St Donatt's Castle in the distance   49

Hokusai: Sekiya Village on the Sumido River   96

Hokusai: Temma Bridge in Osaka   97

John Varley: Snowdon   112

Julius Caesar Ibbetson: Jack in his Glory   113

IN THE TEXT

Aubrey Beardsley: On Dieppe Beach. Drawing *Page* 81

George Cruikshank: 'The Cat did It'. Etching   84

Albrecht Dürer: A Rhinoceros. Woodcut   89

Rembrandt van Rijn: A Young Woman Reading. Etching   98

Acknowledgement is made to the Victoria and Albert Museum, London, for permission to reproduce the following pictures in its collection: *Madame du Barry*, Richard Cosway; *On the Dogger Bank*, by Clarkson Stanfield; *Bulls Fighting*, by James Ward; the two prints by Hokusai; *Snowden*, by John Varley; and *Jack in his Glory*, by J. C. Ibbetson. To the Trustees of the National Gallery, London, for permission to reproduce *Flowerpiece*, by P. J. Van Brussel and to the Trustees of the National Portrait Gallery, London, for permission to reproduce the portrait of Leslie Howard by R. G. Eves.

COLLECTING PICTURES

1

PICTURES FOR PLEASURE

THE FORSYTE family, immortalized by that fashionable novelist John Galsworthy, included picture buyers of two distinct and irreconcilable kinds. Do you remember how James Forsyte, owner of a house in Park Lane, acquires a monstrous Dutch canvas at Jobsons' sale rooms?

' "What—no bid for the Hondekoeter? This large masterpiece."

'James gazed at the enormous picture on the easel, supported at either end by an attendant. The huge affair was full of poultry and feathers floating in a bit of water and a large white rooster looking as if it were about to take a bath. It was a dark painting, save for the rooster, with a yellowish tone.

' "Come, gentlemen? By a celebrated painter of domestic poultry. May I say fifty? Forty? Who'll give me forty pounds? It's giving it away. Well, thirty to start it? Look at the rooster! Masterly painting! Come now! I'll take any bid."

' "Five pounds!" said James, covering the words so that no one but the auctioneer should see where they came from.

' "Five pounds for this genuine work by a master of domestic poultry! Ten pounds did you say, sir? Ten pounds bid."

' "Fifteen," muttered James.

" 'Twenty."

" 'Twenty-five," said James; but he was not going above thirty.

' "Twenty-five—why, the frame's worth it. Who says thirty?"

'No one said thirty; and the picture was knocked down to James, whose mouth had opened slightly. He hadn't meant to buy it; but the thing was a bargain—the size had frightened

13

them; Jolyon had paid one hundred and forty for his Hondekoeter. Well, it would cover that blank on the stairs.'

And there is James's son Soames, who is fatally injured by a
falling copy of Goya's *Vendimia* just after he has rescued his
favourite paintings from the blazing gallery at his home at
Mapledurham. Soames is a fine example of the kind of man
who is as fond of his pictures as he is of his friends. His
Constable, his Alfred Stevens, his Corot and his Daumier are
an unfailing source of pleasure to him, and he turns to them
for solace whenever the worries of the political situation, his
investments, or the members of his family are more than he
can bear. How is it that pictures can play so important a part
in anyone's life?

   To answer that question adequately, we have to know
something about the origins of drawing and painting, and
the other graphic arts.

   The earliest artists whose work still survives were cave
dwellers, in palaeolithic times. They used charred sticks and
red earths to draw on the curved surfaces of their rocky
shelters the wild animals they knew so well, and on which
they depended for a large part of their food and clothing.
Possibly, their work had some magical significance—they
may have intended their pictures to give them increased
power over the elusive beasts they chose to represent. No
one who has ever been to see the famous cave paintings at
Lascaux in the South of France can have come away unmoved
by the fantastically accurate observation of the primitive
hunter-artists who worked there so many centuries ago.

   In the Middle Ages, most European artists learned their
trade by being apprenticed to some established master—
there were no Art Schools, as there are today—and the vast
majority of the great works of art that have survived from
those days were produced under the aegis of the Church.
That does not mean that all medieval artists were necessarily
devout, but their subject-matter, if not their treatment of it,
was almost inevitably religious.

   The idea that pictures were a desirable form of private
property and could be bought or exchanged and collected did

not really gain ready acceptance until the great Italian families such as the Medicis and the Sforzas extended their munificent patronage to the towering figures of the Renaissance: Michelangelo, Leonardo da Vinci, Raphael Santi and their contemporaries. Since that time it has been regarded as entirely natural that there shall be pictures in every civilized home. But they don't hang on the walls to make hunting easier, and a lot of them have no religious significance whatsoever. The vast majority have been collected solely to give pleasure—and that, surely, is the very best reason for acquiring and living with pictures.

But there are some other reasons for collecting pictures, too, that are worth our consideration.

We all know the enormous advantages we get from our sense of sight, as long as it is working properly, and the onerous handicaps we suffer when our vision becomes defective, or, worse, if it fails altogether. Pictorial artists (by those words we may mean draughtsmen, etchers, engravers and lithographers, as well as straightforward painters) are people who have learned to use their eyes more efficiently and with a greater sense of purpose than the rest of the community. By collecting pictures, and by giving them the prolonged and intensive study that is only possible when we have them in our own homes, we can acquire at second hand some of the 'extra' vision of an artist, or of several artists. While it would not be true to say that Claude Lorraine or Turner invented sunsets, it is certain that we appreciate the golden glow of an evening sky more readily if we have seen and 'digested' the radiant canvases of those most accomplished artists. We tend to see, in fact, what the great masters have shown us, rather than what we can see for ourselves.

A look back over the history of painting is, for the picture enthusiast, as stimulating and satisfying as a review of past meals is for the gourmet. It may be salutary to consider briefly at this point some of the great artists of the past who can fairly be said to have contributed most to our outlook today. You may never be able to afford any original works by any of these artists, but the influence of at least one of them will be evident in every picture you hang on your walls.

The first figure of any lasting importance in the history of European painting is, most authorities would say, the great Italian artist Giotto di Bondone (1266 or 7–1337). There were other notable painters before him, of course—the rigidly decorative works of Duccio di Buoninsegna (1255–1318) and of Margarito of Arezzo (known to have been active *c.* 1262) may evoke a certain feeling of reverence in the present-day gallery-goer, if nothing else—but Giotto brought the human figure to life in his paintings in a way that made the stiff Madonnas and formalized Holy Children of his contemporaries seem like two-dimensional dolls. Giotto is inseparably connected in our minds with St Francis of Assisi, and much of the divine simplicity of that miraculous person may be said to have rubbed off on the artist who depicted the most important episodes in the saint's eventful life.

The creative explosion sparked off by Giotto's achievements was far-reaching in its effects. While Paolo Uccello (1397–1475) and the brothers Pollaiuolo (died 1496 and 1498) were carrying out invaluable research into the principles of linear perspective and human anatomy respectively, and while Masaccio (1401–1428) and Piero della Francesca (1420–1492) were washing monumental masterpieces directly into the fresh plaster of extensive Italian walls and ceilings, artists in the Low Countries were bringing the microscopically detailed approach of the Northern European manuscript illuminators as close as possible to perfection. Robert Campin (1378–1444), Hubert and Jan Van Eyck (1385–1441), Rogier Van der Weyden (1400–1464) and Hans Memling (1430–1494) packed an almost miraculous amount of significant detail into every square centimetre of their relatively small easel pictures, and opened people's eyes to the richness and variety of the surface textures that surround us in our everyday life.

The beginning of the sixteenth century saw some of the greatest masters of the Renaissance well launched on their busy careers. Leonardo da Vinci (1452–1519), as great a scientist as he was an artist, was exploring the full resources of light and shade, or 'chiaroscuro'; Michelangelo Buonarroti (1475–1564), one of the world's most impressive sculptors as well as being an architect, painter and poet, was using the male form as a symbol of supernatural power; and Raphael Santi (1483–1520) was combining all the pictorial discoveries of his predecessors in compositions of sublime authority. Never before or since has such a galaxy of artists been working in one country on so many projects of such transcendental importance.

Meanwhile, in Flanders, Pieter Breughel the Elder was working on a slightly larger scale than most of his compatriots. It is not surprising that his canvases have been respected by the experts as well as being loved by the members of the lay public for more than four hundred years. He subjected village weddings, children's games, the pastoral activities of the peasant and the sadder manifestations of the Spanish Inquisition to the same wonderfully observant scrutiny, and his paintings combine the exquisite colour and detail of his Netherlandish forebears with the power and inventiveness of the great Italian mural decorators.

Venetian painting was, from the earliest days, quite splendidly sumptuous. Situated at the head of the Adriatic, this great port has always acted as a funnel through which the exotic wares and products of the East have passed on their way to the markets of Europe. Jacopo Bellini (1400–1470), Gentile Bellini (1429–1507), Giovanni Bellini (1430–1516), Giorgione (1478–1510) and Titian (1490–1576) were the founder figures of a school which included such magnificent colourists as Jacopo Robusti or 'Tintoretto' (1518–1604) and Veronese (1528–1588). There was a brief after-flowering a hundred years or so later when Giovanni Battista Tiepolo (1696–1770), Antonio Canale or 'Canaletto' (1697–1768) and Francesco Guardi (1712–1793) captured, each in his own individual way, the charm of their lovely city.

The seventeenth century might be described as a period of consolidation, when the great pioneering work done by the innovators of the Seicento produced its richest harvest. It gave us Rembrandt van Rijn (1606–1669) for instance, the incomparable Dutchman whose portraits are more than representations of men and women—they are profound statements about the whole human comedy, or tragedy, whichever you

2

think it should be called. The number of people in the world who can add a genuine Rembrandt to a collection is obviously limited—a tiny self-portrait 8 in. by 6¾ in. changed hands for £36,500 in Paris in 1965—but there are many minor portrait painters of the eighteenth and early nineteenth centuries who reflect in a subdued way a little at least of his genius, having inherited or acquired some of his extraordinary insight into character. You can still see genuine examples of their work in undisturbed country houses, and they come on to the market whenever there is a dispersal sale.

Two other towering figures of the seventeenth century came from north-west Europe—Sir Peter Paul Rubens (1577–1640) and Sir Anthony Van Dyck (1599–1641). They may truly be said to have developed, if they did not actually initiate, the 'Grand Manner', that supremely flattering way of showing aristocratic personages at their most elegant, in surroundings of the utmost grandeur. Again, you may never have the chance to own an original Rubens or Van Dyck unless you are lucky enough to inherit one, but you may easily pick up a small canvas by some late Georgian journeyman painter who learned his craft with one eye on those masters, and who captured in his work some of the orderliness and charm of a supremely civilized age.

With the eighteenth century, we move into a period that tends to interest the picture collector above all others—chiefly because many of the works produced in it reflect the general style and graciousness of the era without being so rare or so precious that they can be normally encountered only in the slightly impersonal atmosphere of the great public galleries and museums. In Britain, the second Augustan age produced William Hogarth, whom we shall consider in more detail in the chapter that deals with engraving; Richard Wilson (1714–1782), the father of English landscape painting, whose golden-brown canvases evoke for us the atmosphere of classical serenity with which Wilson became familiar while he was spending his formative years in Italy; and Thomas Gainsborough (1727–1788), the great portrait painter, and his eminent rival Sir Joshua Reynolds (1723–1792): while in France artists as various as Jean Antoine Watteau (1684–

1721), François Boucher (1703–1770), and Jean Honoré Fragonard drew their inspiration from the gay but slightly feverish pleasure-seeking of a highly cultivated and doomed aristocracy.

During the first and second decades of the nineteenth century, an extraordinary number of prolific and highly talented artists were working in Britain. There was William Blake (1757–1827) for instance, whose attitude to his native land can be judged from the words of *Jerusalem*:

> *And did those feet in ancient time*
> *Walk upon England's mountains green,*
> *And was the Holy Lamb of God*
> *On England's pleasant pastures seen?*

and whose ideas about painting can be best assessed from a few quotations from his occasional writings:

'In a work of Art it is not Fine Tints that are required, but Fine Forms; fine Tints without, are nothing. Fine Tints without Fine Forms are always the Subterfuge of the Blockhead.'

'No man of Sense can think that an Imitation of the Objects of Nature is the Art of Painting, or that such Imitation, which anyone may easily perform, is worthy of Notice, much less that such an Art should be the Glory & Pride of a Nation.'

'The difference between a bad Artist & a Good One Is: the Bad Artist Seems to copy a Great deal. The Good one Really does Copy a Great deal.'

While Blake was reproducing the strange images of his inner vision at London and Felpham, Joseph Mallord William Turner (1775–1851) was travelling over much of Britain and parts of the Continent with his eyes turned resolutely outwards. Turner was possibly more aware of the weather than any other artist who has ever lived in any country. Like King Lear, he could see the whole of human experience in a thunderstorm, all life in a shower of rain. Towards the end of his career, the storms and the rain tended to wash most of the land out of his landscapes, leaving only the rough weather

behind, but there is no doubt that his work has been so great
an influence on later painters that he might even be referred
to as the 'First of the Moderns'.

John Constable was born the year after Turner, but died
fourteen years before him. Constable's paintings of Suffolk
harvest fields and riverside meadows seem pleasant and harmless enough to us now, but they were considered quite revolutionary when they first brought the fresh strong colours of the
English countryside to the notice of the picture-buying public.
'I constantly observe that every man who will not submit to
long toil in the imitation of nature, flies off, becomes a
phantom, and produces dreams of nonsense and abortions,'
wrote Constable, and in the best of his sketches he has repro-
duced perfectly the shimmering play of sunlight as it falls on
breeze-swept vegetation.

The third and fourth decades of the nineteenth century saw
the development of the camera and with it the artist's release
from one form of bondage: no longer would it be almost
obligatory for him to reproduce the natural world in easily
comprehensible terms—the photographer's magic box could
record the outward physical appearance of people and places
much more quickly and accurately than any fallible human
being. From that time on, the painter has tended to regard
his own work as a form of research, and the critics and dealers
have tended to assess its value in direct proportion to its
originality. So, let us look next at some of the 'isms' that
have followed one another during the past hundred years with
such bewildering rapidity.

First, Impressionism, which was developed in France by
a group of painters who were primarily concerned with
rendering faithfully the transitory effects of atmosphere and
light. Even people who consider themselves allergic to
modern art are usually ready to be enchanted by the sunlit
gardenscapes of Claude Monet (1840–1926) and Camille
Pissarro (1831–1903), the riverside scenes of Alfred Sisley
(1839–1899), and the porcelain-like figure studies of Pierre
Auguste Renoir (1841–1919). Germain Edgar Hilaire Degas
(1834–1917) was too independent a figure to allow himself to
be classified with any group or school, but his sketches of the

ballet are perhaps the most exciting theatrical pictures that have ever been produced or ever will be produced.

Post-Impressionism is not quite so easy to define as Impressionism, as it was a movement dominated by a small handful of men with strong personalities and widely divergent styles. It is difficult for the untrained eye to see any common denominator in the paintings of Paul Cézanne (1839–1906), Vincent Van Gogh (1853–1890) and Paul Gauguin (1848–1903), but there are few artists who have done any work worth looking at in the past fifty years who have not been influenced by their insistence on the architectural organization of a picture, and their masterly control of form.

The Cubists, set on their way by Georges Braque and Pablo Picasso, found new and exciting ways of analysing or synthesizing solid shapes; the Fauves or 'Wild Beasts', whose pictures are anything but pretty yet usually exercise a strange fascination on anyone who studies them; the Futurists who tried to suggest violent movement and the passage of time on inert, two-dimensional surfaces; the Surrealists, who explored the strange and disturbing recesses of the subconscious mind—all these groups who seemed so revolutionary when their work first entered the galleries began to seem quite staid and respectable during the artistic maelstroms of the 'fifties and 'sixties. In the last two decades, Action Painting has been followed by Abstract Expressionism, and that has been superseded by the New Figuration, Pop Art, the Art of Optical Illusion, and Kinetic Art in rapid succession. Already, the second half of the twentieth century has produced so many changes of trend and reversals of attitude that it is unsafe for any chronicler to try to put them in their correct order.

The history of painting, then, allows plenty of scope for the collector who wishes to specialize. If you want to enjoy the pictures on your walls without having to make too much mental effort, you can confine your attentions, say, to the works of the topographical artists of the eighteenth and nineteenth centuries and to comparable representational painters. If you find traditional or figurative art a trifle tedious, you can build up an exciting display of abstract pictures painted in the past ten years. Only a comparatively daring and

knowledgeable authority can mix successfully in one single
collection the works of a large number of different artists, of
unrelated styles and outlooks, who lived at various times over
a period of several centuries.

You may have noticed how the curators of the world's
great galleries tend to hang together in groups the works of
the artists who were associated with each other when they
were alive. By doing this these curators avoid the disturbing
effect of miscellany which can result when too many pictures
that are completely unlike are mixed up in a haphazard way,
and instead they emphasize the threads of historical con-
tinuity that give so much additional interest to the works
entrusted to their care. In a private collection, the unifying
element may be the personal taste of the collector.

The pleasure and enlightenment that may be expected
from a collection of pictures have already been mentioned.
There is a third reason for acquiring them which may or may
not interest you, according to your nature—chosen wisely,
they make an excellent form of investment. We are probably
safe in taking it for granted nowadays that money tucked
away for safety under the floor will decline progressively in
purchasing power as the years roll on. Works of art, antique
furniture, fine silver and precious jewels are more likely to
appreciate in value. Many rich people, then, collect pictures
as a bulwark against inflation. But if you decide to follow
their example, don't forget the operative words 'chosen
wisely', for artists' reputations can be inflated temporarily
out of all proportion to their work's true worth. A painting
by Sir Edwin Landseer (1802–1873), which would have cost
several thousand pounds in the artist's lifetime, can be bought
for a few hundreds today. Backing bad artists can be as
disastrous, financially, as backing bad horses.

It is not surprising that we tend to hear more about the
successful picture collectors than about the people who are
sold the traditional 'pups'—the latter usually do all they can
to avoid publicity.

Let us look next at some of the great collectors who have
earned fame as much by the number and quality of the works
of art they have acquired as by their wealth or achievements.

First, there are the men and women whose property has passed, after their death, to form the nucleus of some great national collection. One of the most notable of these was the wealthy Russian merchant John Julius Angerstein who settled in England around the year 1749. He was an assiduous purchaser of pictures and had an uncommonly keen nose for a cheap masterpiece. After his death, the British Government took thirty-eight of his pictures, including the six scenes of Hogarth's *Marriage-à-la-Mode* and five splendid landscapes by Claude Lorraine, paying for them by a vote of £60,000, and founding by that transaction the National Gallery that is so universally admired today.

Just as enthusiastic, and even more catholic in his tastes was Sir Richard Wallace, to whom Britain owes the splendours of the Wallace Collection. Born in 1818, the natural son of the fourth Marquess of Hertford and one Agnes Jackson, he spent much of the prime of his life in Paris, helping his father to acquire the magnificent collection of paintings, armour, furniture and *objets d'art* that now bears his name. In 1870 the Marquess died, bequeathing the collection to his son. It passed to the nation in 1897 on the death of Sir Richard Wallace's widow, and may still be visited at Hertford House, Manchester Square, London W 1.

Fortunately for artists and dealers, there have been a few collectors operating on the same munificent scale during the twentieth century. Mr Pierpoint Morgan, for instance, made a habit of going through Italy, buying from obscure and impoverished noblemen the masterpieces that are now among the treasures of the Metropolitan Museum, New York. Alfred Barnes, the Philadelphia manufacturer who became world famous by the ruthless way in which he collected the paintings of Cézanne, is another example. And how can one think without a small pang of envy of the good fortune of people like Mr and Mrs Robert Lehman, also of New York, who can feast their eyes as they sit at ease in their drawing-room on two magnificent Rembrandts and a pair of El Grecos, as well as many other almost priceless works of art?

One widely believed fallacy must be scotched here, now, right at the beginning of this book—it is *not* necessary to be enormously wealthy to become a collector of pictures. Obviously, the people who bid to astronomic figures at Sotheby's and Christies' sale rooms are more likely to be property magnates or oil kings than old age pensioners, but for every enlightened tycoon who collects pictures on those exalted levels there are scores of picture-owners who lay out less in a year than the average smoker spends on tobacco. People who buy pictures on this modest scale may not finish with collections as transcendentally valuable as those of J. J. Angerstein, J. Pierpoint Morgan, or any one of a dozen Rothschilds, but their purchases may give them almost ceaseless interest and happiness. And what finer yield can any of us ask from our investments than that?

2

HOW TO HANG, LIGHT AND STORE PICTURES

JUST AS a philatelist will spend many enjoyable hours planning the layout of his stamps on the pages of an album, so you, as a picture collector, will get a lot of pleasure from the time you spend arranging and hanging your treasures. You will constantly find yourself faced with fresh problems of presentation and display, but these can be easily solved with a minimum of technical know-how.

The first step to be taken sounds easy—you simply have to find a wall or walls that you can use to support your pictures, and to act as a background for them. But not all walls are equally suitable. A wall that contains a large window may be rather too dark, especially when the sun is shining outside. A wall that faces a large window may be almost as ungenerous to pictures, since the light from outside will probably be reflected from glazed or varnished surfaces, to distract with its shine or glare. Walls set at right angles to the wall that contains the main source of light are usually the best for pictures, but each room has to be judged separately and assessed on its individual merits after a certain amount of experiment. A room with a ceiling light may be splendid for hanging on all four sides.

Having decided which of the walls at your disposal will be suitable for the display of your collection, you will next have to make sure that the walls you have chosen are suitably 'decorated'—if that is the right word to use, for the plainer the background to a picture, in normal circumstances, the better. To reduce the colour of a wall to a less powerful shade or tint, or to knock out an aggressive pattern you may have to apply a coat of neutral paint or distemper. If it is not convenient for you to do that, you can change the appearance

25

of a place satisfactorily by hanging large sheets of hessian, sailcloth, tarpaulin or other fabrics over the surfaces on which the pictures are to be arranged.

Next, you will have to decide how you are going to keep your pictures in the positions you choose for them. Most paintings can be suspended safely by means of the closed rings sold specially for the purpose, which can be screwed into the backs of the frames. If you insert these rings near the top of the frame the picture will hang straight down. If you insert them two or three inches from the top the picture will tend to tilt forward at a slight angle. Experiment, to find out which method you prefer.

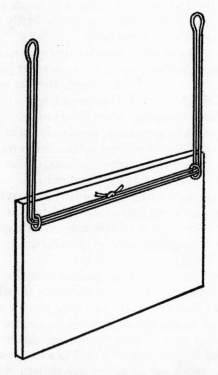

1. A running loop used for hanging
pictures

You can choose, too, whether you are going to use string, picture cord, wire or fine chain for hanging your pictures. Only the smallest and lightest pictures can be hung from a single nail fixing. If you are hanging a picture from two points you can tie the two ends of a length of picture cord together and you can use the resulting double thickness as a running loop, as shown in Fig. 1. This is a very useful way of suspending pictures, as they can be re-aligned by a touch of the finger if they are out of true.

If your walls are fitted with picture rails, you can use hangers of the conventional type for suspending your pictures. If they are of the modern flush type, you will have to use some alternative method of suspension. Here are two suggestions:

(a) You can fix strips of wood to the walls so that they look like horizontal bands running round your gallery a foot or so apart. Ordinary wood screws fixed in the back of the frames can then be made to engage in, or rest on, these strips so that the pictures rest snugly against the walls, and are easy to keep level.

(b) You can fix a metal tube or strip along the top of each wall, near the ceiling. Chains can then be hung from this lofty horizontal datum line to provide an easy side-to-side and up-and-down adjustment.

Should the walls of your 'gallery' be lined with wood or some similar material, you can screw small pierced plates to the backs of the frames. Then you can ask someone to hold the pictures in position while you screw the plates to the wall.

Here's a tip that you may find useful when you are trying to decide which of your pictures to put on any wall, and how to arrange the ones you have chosen—lay them flat on the floor, first, and move them around there. Make up your mind at the earliest possible moment about the pictures that are to hang in the centre of the wall, and then try various other pictures, on each side of the centrepiece, so that the whole group makes a pleasing and balanced composition. When you are certain that the arrangement cannot be improved, it is a simple matter to transfer the pictures from the floor into the corresponding positions on the wall.

And here are a few pitfalls to avoid:

Overcrowded walls are rarely satisfactory. Many eminent Victorians had a habit of covering every available square inch of wall space with a picture of some kind. They produced some splendidly opulent interiors by these methods, but the whole effect was usually overpowering, and did not encourage a detailed study of any individual work. James McNeill Whistler, sweeping away the cobwebby ideas of a generation he despised, showed us how a single picture placed perfectly on a wall can be a source of genuine aesthetic satisfaction.

Pictures that are hanging too high to be viewed in comfort are wasted. You cannot hope to be able to give any picture a worth while scrutiny unless you can look at it with a straight level gaze.

Pictures hanging at a number of different levels on a wall may not be very pleasing to the eye. Try arranging a row of pictures of differing sizes so that the lowest edge of the frame of each is exactly the same height (say, 3 ft. 6 in.) from the floor. Pictures lined up in this way will usually be an asset to the decorative scheme of a room, even though their frames may be of various heights, weights and colours.

Picture collectors can usually be roughly divided into two categories—those who tend to leave their pictures in the same positions on their walls for years and years, and those who like shuffling their pictures around periodically so that they make a fresh impact when seen in new surroundings. There is a lot to be said for each of those points of view.

If you happen to be one of the people who prefer to leave pictures alone once they have been satisfactorily arranged, you can give special emphasis to any items in your collection that you think merit extra attention by arranging individual lighting for each. Small shaded strip lights can be obtained in fittings that do not obtrude on the view. These throw a soft even beam over a wide area and illuminate a picture in a most flattering way.

As your collection of pictures increases, you may not have room on your walls at any one time for all your accessions ('accessions' is a rather grand word professional curators use to describe the treasures they acquire). Then, the question of safe storage will arise, and this will be especially important if you want to pack away valuable pictures in glazed frames or oil paintings on stretched canvases which can be easily damaged if they are pressed too tightly together.

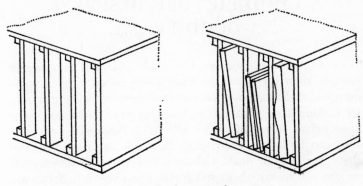

2. A picture rack

The best resting-place for idle pictures is undoubtedly a rack like the one shown in Fig. 2. If you are even moderately useful with your hands, you should be able to construct a rack of this kind, given the necessary pieces of wood, in a single morning or afternoon.

3

A GOOD PICTURE DESERVES
A GOOD FRAME

JUST AS a well-proportioned house is enhanced by a lovely garden, or a fine jewel is made more effective by a well-designed setting, so a good picture deserves the right frame. In making sure that the pictures in your collection have appropriate surrounds, you will have three alternatives—they can be left in the frames in which you have acquired them, they can be dealt with by a professional frame maker, or you can mount them and frame them yourself if you are moderately handy (and if you want to save money). In this chapter, you will find some general remarks about the types of surround suitable for the most commonly encountered kinds of picture, followed by brief notes about the methods you can use for making these surrounds.

MOUNTING PICTURES

Most drawings, water colours, engravings, etchings and lithographs look more attractive if they are isolated from their surroundings by a broad band of neutral material that is usually known as a 'mount'. Mounts can be bought ready made, or they can be prepared from any suitably large sheet of stiff paper or card, but if you decide to give a picture a dark surround, don't let it be so wide that the effect is overwhelming.

One important point is borne in mind by professional framers when they are arranging a picture on a mount—almost invariably, they make the margin below the picture a little wider than any of the others. This is shown in Fig. 3. If you are doing the job yourself, find the most pleasing position for the picture and then mark the outlines of the

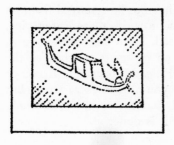

3. A picture needs to be placed satisfactorily on a mount

corners with a faint right angle or cross. Then you will be able to put the picture back in exactly the same place when you have dealt with the problem of fixing it in position.

There are innumerable glues, pastes and sticky strips that can be used for mounting pictures which are of no particular financial value, and are likely to remain of no particular value, such as photographs, reproductions and children's sketches. A 'cold' glue is especially useful, its main advantages being the slowness with which the adhesive sets and the absence, therefore, of any great need to hurry.

When you are mounting a picture of this sort, put it face downwards on a piece of scrap paper and spread the adhesive out from the middle and over the edges, as shown in Fig. 4. You will find it useful to have a piece of clean cloth handy when you do this in case you accidentally get any adhesive on the front surface of the picture.

If the paper on which the picture is drawn or printed is reasonably thin and pliable, you should be able to rub away without much difficulty any wrinkles or blisters caused by trapped air. Leave the picture to dry for a few hours under a flat piece of wood such as a drawing board, or, even better, under a clean sheet of glass. Then hold the mount up and decide if it needs any embellishment.

It would be unwise, for obvious reasons, to apply any considerable quantity of adhesive to the back of any precious picture, or one that is likely to have to be removed from its surround at any time. For pictures in these categories, bevelled mounts are normally used. With these, the pictures are set behind the boards instead of being attached to the front surfaces—the sloping bevels neatly concealing the outer edges. Cutting bevels will give you a little extra work, but if you are careful you will find that the results will amply justify the trouble. This is how it is done:

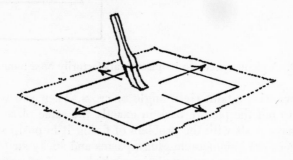

4. Spreading adhesive

When you have found the most satisfactory position for a picture, locate its corners by making faint pencil marks on the mount. Then take the picture away and join the corner-marks so that you have drawn a rectangle on the mount that is exactly the same size as the picture. The four sides of the rectangle will be used for guiding the cutter.

For cutting a bevel you can use a really sharp penknife, a new steel-backed razor blade, an X-Acto knife, or some other keen implement. (It is not safe to use an ordinary two-edged razor blade.) Put the mount on a sheet of thick glass, on a metal plate, or on some other hard flat supporting surface. Then put a steel rule or some other metal straight-edge on the mount in such a way that you can cut along each of the guide lines with your knife or blade at an angle of 45°, as shown in Fig. 5. Try to cut right through the mount, if you can, with one movement of the blade. If you are forced to make a second cut you may find yourself paring off thin slices of card that curl up like bacon rind.

Flowerpiece by P. J. Van Brussel: a flower picture can bring brightness
into the home on the dullest day

Leslie Howard by R. G. Eves: the portraits on this page would give life and interest to any wall

Madame Du Barry: an unfinished miniature by Richard Cosway, R.A., painted in 1791

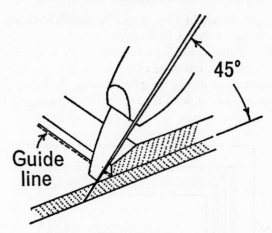

5. Cutting a bevel through a mount

If you cut your bevels carefully, you will find, when you have completed all four, that only a very small part of the picture surface will be hidden by the mount. Small pieces of gummed strip or stamp hinges can be used for holding the picture in its allotted position.

RULED AND TINTED MOUNTS

A plain white, buff or pale grey mount will suit most pictures (other than oil paintings) admirably, but ruled and tinted mounts can be used to give a really luxurious appearance to a collection. In Fig. 6 you can see how the surface of one of

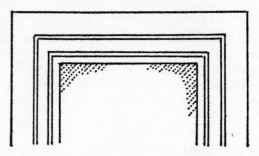

6. A ruled mount

the mounts shown in Fig. 3 can be subdivided with ruled straight lines so that a decorative inner border is produced round the picture. Borders of this kind add interest and variety to mounts, but need to be neatly and accurately done. Pencils or crayons can be used for drawing them, and ink lines can be made to look dead true with a ruling pen and straight edge.

7. A tinted mount

If the picture you are framing is one of which you are particularly fond, so that a little extra effort is justified, you may care to add a band of tone or colour to the decorative surround just described. To do this, paint the space between two sets of parallel lines with water colour or diluted ink, using a fine sable brush so that you can control the wash-in exactly. A tinted mount is shown in Fig. 7.

PASSE-PARTOUT FRAMES

One of the easiest and cheapest ways of framing pictures at home is provided by the special gummed strips known usually as passe-partout. These are marketed in a wide range of colours and finishes, and can be obtained at most stationers' shops. No one could claim very convincingly that passe-partout frames are substantial enough to lend dignity to pictures on permanent display, but as a means of providing temporary protection to easily soiled or damaged surfaces they can be heartily recommended.

Let us suppose that you wish to frame a picture for which you have already bought or made a bevelled mount. First, you will need to find a piece of picture glass and a strong smooth backing board, which may be hardboard, plywood, thick cardboard, or any other reasonably rigid material. Both the glass and the backing board should be exactly the same size as the mount. It will save a lot of trouble if you fix on a size that will suit any materials that you may have available.

If you have to reduce the size of a sheet of glass to suit a mount that is already determined, you can use a diamond cutter if you have one, or one of the reasonably satisfactory wheel cutters that are sold at most ironmongers' and hardware stores. It is not a particularly difficult job, but if you are a novice you may prefer to ask someone who has had some previous experience to do the actual cutting for you.

If you are going to cut the glass yourself, put it on a soft thick cloth, or on several thicknesses of newspaper, on a firm table or workbench. Mark off the cutting line with a ruler or straight-edge, and then, using that as a guide, run the glass-cutter along so that it breaks the invisible 'outer skin' of the glass as it travels. Then move the glass so that the line you have cut is parallel to, and a fraction of an inch away from, the edge of the table or workbench, and so that the piece you wish to remove has no visible means of support. If you then give the underside of the glass a series of sharp taps with the back of your cutter, directly beneath the scribed line, you should find that a clean, straight fracture will result, exactly where you want it.

Before you assemble the glass, the mount, the picture and the backing board in their final positions, polish the glass and insert in the backing board any tapes or rings you may need for hanging the picture. Cut slits where these are to be, and if you are using loops of tape push the ends through and glue them to the underside of the backing. If you are using the specially manufactured picture rings which have a circle of wire and two flat metal tongues, push these tongues through the slits and bend them apart. A square of passe-partout can be used to cover any unsightly ends and make a really neat job.

Next, assemble the various components in their correct relative positions and hold them together temporarily with Bulldog clips or sprung clothes pegs while you get the passe-partout edging ready.

Most passe-partout bindings sold nowadays are scored ready for use, by the manufacturers, and when you have cut off four lengths, each half an inch or so longer than the side of the glass that it is to cover, you will be able to bend them over without any difficulty into the positions they are to occupy. Try them in place before you moisten the adhesive on the back. Once you have damped the pieces of strip you will find them most inconveniently sticky. And that brings us to one of the really important things to remember about passe-partout: if you use plenty of water, and if you make sure that the whole layer of adhesive is thoroughly moistened, the strip will stay in position almost indefinitely. If you do the job in a hurry you may find that the binding, after a little time, peels away from the glass.

As soon as the first strip is ready, put it sticky side upwards on your working surface. Pick up the picture and lay the appropriate edge on the binding between the creases you have already made, then fold the outer strips over on to the front and back of the picture and press every part of the binding into position as firmly as you can. Next apply the second

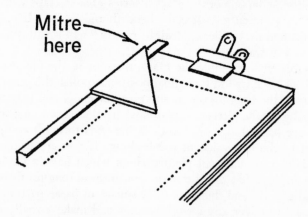

8. Trimming passe-partout strip

strip to the side of the picture that is parallel to the side you have already bound. You will have to leave the two sides that are at right angles to these until you have made the first mitres at the corners.

To trim the corners, you will need a 45° set square and a very sharp knife or a steel-backed razor blade. Use the set square to guide the cutting edge, as shown in Fig. 8. When you remove the surplus trimmings of binding you may pull the other pieces away from the glass. If this happens you can easily remedy the damage by re-moistening the accessible adhesive and by pressing the loose material back into position until the adhesive has set.

Now you can apply strips of binding to the remaining sides of the picture. Trim these strips carefully so that their ends fit exactly against the preliminary mitres you have already cut. Then leave the picture in a moderately warm place for a few hours so that the binding can dry out thoroughly, give the glass a final polish, and the frame will be complete.

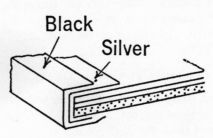

Black

Silver

9. Two colours used in a passe-partout
frame

If you want to make an especially decorative frame—as, for instance, if you have a print that calls for a rather special surround—you can quite easily combine two or more strips of passe-partout of different colours, and the effect produced may be both satisfying and rich.

Fig. 9 shows how a strip of black passe-partout can be superimposed on a strip of silver so that a thin band of silver is left exposed. In Fig. 10 you can see how strips of straw-board or cardboard can be used to build up a frame that looks

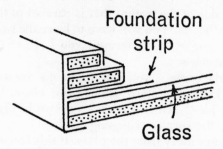

10. Building up a passe-partout frame

almost as solid as a wooden moulding. A firm foundation for a built-up frame can be provided by cementing a strip of plain passe-partout directly on to the glass with its own adhesive. On that base, strips of strawboard or cardboard, that have been already covered with passe-partout and mitred, can be assembled with Evo-stik or some similar ready-to-use adhesive. You can combine several strips of board, if you wish, to give extra thickness. But don't put too much pressure on any sheet of picture glass, in one of these frame-building operations, or it will almost certainly crack.

FRAMES FOR OIL-PAINTINGS

Unfortunately, passe-partout and similar frames are much too slight to make good surrounds for oil-paintings, which need to be separated from the background around them by more substantial mouldings. If the cost of buying ready-made frames for the oil paintings in your collection does not prove prohibitive, you will find your shopping expeditions quite stimulating.

However good the frame-maker you patronize, you will need to use a lot of taste and judgement when you are purchasing his wares. Frames are so infinitely various—they range from the plain, thin, simple mouldings that are ideal for water-colours to the swirling, rococo concoctions seen usually round the works of the more frivolous French boudoir decorators. One of your tasks will be selecting the type of frame that suits each of the items in your collection—frames with pleasantly curved corners for your landscapes, perhaps; frames with dignified straight mouldings for formal portraits. A good painting can be spoiled by a badly chosen frame.

Often you can find frames in second-hand goods shops that are perfectly adequate and much cheaper than new frames. If parts of the moulding of a second-hand frame have been knocked away you can build up the gaps with plastic wood, Alabastine, Polyfilla, or any one of the dozens of proprietary cements now on the market.

If you want to 'strip' old second-hand frames so that you can replace the heavy gold or thick colour with a surface of your own choice, you will find a solution of caustic soda useful. Wear rubber gloves when you are using this or any other powerful stripping agent, to protect your hands, and be careful to wash every trace of the stripper away before you add any fresh texturing or colour.

If you are a handy person, or if you can persuade a reasonably handy person to work for you, you can make your own frames at a fraction of their commercial cost.

First, you will need to obtain some lengths of wooden moulding of a suitable section. Inexpensive mouldings can be bought at most timber yards and from many builders' merchants.

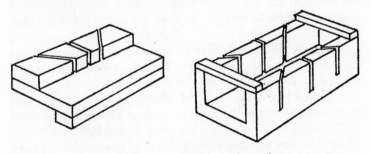

11. Appliances used for cutting mitres

Then you will need a set of mitre-blocks, or a mitre-box. These appliances, which are shown in Fig. 11, are used for sawing the corner surfaces correctly at an angle of 45° to the main run of the frame. You will also need a small vice and a glue-pot, and the few tools such as a hammer and an X-Acto knife that are to be found in any home workshop.

Mitred corners have to be cut and joined carefully if the frame is not to look an absolute wreck. Most craftsmen like to assemble their frames with strong glue, clamping the parts of each corner tightly together until the adhesive has had plenty of time to set. Usually, fine nails or panel pins are used to complete each joint.

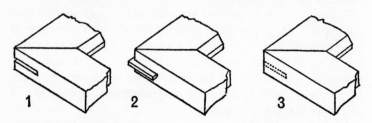

12. Veneer used to give strength to a mitred joint

Sometimes, a careful craftsman will give extra strength to a mitred joint by inserting a piece of glued veneer into a saw-cut he has made through the two adjoining pieces [Fig. 12]. The veneer, which should be a firm 'push fit' in the saw-slit, can be trimmed back with a razor blade or a very sharp knife to suit the shape of the frame when the glue is dry.

There are dozens of different methods of finishing frames once they have been made up. You can paint them, polish them, coat them with 'gesso' (slaked plaster, in a weak solution of glue) or with size and whiting, gild them, burnish them, cover them with cloths of various kinds, stipple them with torn-up newspaper that has been dipped into decorators' colours, or any combination of these. If the mouldings used are of a particularly choice wood, they can be left as they are, with the natural grain setting off the richer textures of the paint surface and canvas.

Many artists like to lay several coats of colour on each of their frames, choosing these carefully to harmonize with, and set off, the colours in the picture to be accommodated—with, perhaps, a rich Venetian red and a dull gold in the deepest layers. They scrape the frames gently with a sharp knife when all the coats of paint are dry. The underlying colours then come through to the surface in a few places only. Effects of the greatest subtlety can be attained by these means. If you go to any successful picture dealer's gallery you will come away with enough ideas about frames and frame treatments to last you a twelvemonth. It is his business, after all, to keep up with the trend.

4

HOW TO BUILD UP A COLLECTION OF PICTURES WITHOUT GOING BANKRUPT

IN THE first chapter, the point was made that one does not have to be a millionaire before one can build up an admirable collection of pictures. In this chapter, the problems of picture buying are examined in more detail, and so are some of the steps one can take to build up a collection without involving oneself in financial disaster.

The most exhilarating way of buying a picture is undoubtedly to bid for it at an auction sale. There, the true commercial value of an artist's work is established by the dynamic interplay of competitive forces, the final level reached by the bidding being, admittedly, occasionally affected by the skill of the auctioneer, by the wiles of the contestants, or by the highly charged emotional atmosphere. At the world's most famous sale rooms—at Sotheby's and Christies' in London, for instance, and at the Parke-Bernet Galleries in New York—the tensions generated by the intense competition are as full of dramatic interest as any that are ever experienced in a theatre or opera house.

Take, for example, an occasion like that at Sotheby's recently, when an oil-painting that measured just a little over five by four inches was sold for £220,000—that works out at about £11,000 per square inch.

The painting—*St George and the Dragon*, attributed to the mysterious Flemish master Hubert Van Eyck—had attracted to the sale rooms art experts from all over the world. The arrival in the crowded room of the American ambassador and his wife revived rumours that the tiny masterpiece was destined to cross the Atlantic, whatever the price level reached.

It was known that no British public gallery could afford to compete with the most powerful private collectors in the world, most of whom were present, or were represented.

The bidding was started at £20,000—itself a formidable figure to pay for such a tiny picture. Less than two and a quarter minutes later, the auctioneer was eliciting bids ten times as great as that. When his gavel finally fell, 132 seconds after the bidding started, there was a disappointed underbidder who had been prepared to pay £215,000. When the vendor was asked after the sale why she had decided to sell the little painting, which she had inherited from her mother, she is reported to have said, 'I had been afraid for some time that it would be stolen. After all, it is so small that anyone could take it away in a pocket. Also, I realized it would be worth a considerable amount of money.'

Clearly, the proprietors of the sale rooms where such auctions take place would be slow if they did not do everything in their power to attract wealthy patrons—as sellers, as buyers, and as spectators—to their establishments. Recently, it has been made possible by long-distance telegraphy for auctions to be held with the buyers in places many thousands of miles apart. Television cameras, too, have been brought in to make the excitements of a crowded sale room part of an evening's entertainment for the masses. It takes a level-headed man—or woman—to bid intelligently, and to know when to stop bidding, when every decision has to be made in the full close-up view of millions of people.

Local auctions—such as those that take place when the contents of a family home are dispersed—may be a little less embarrassing and hazardous than the sales that attract the international trade, but even at one of these the inexperienced collector may be roused into paying an uneconomic price for a picture by collusive action on the part of the dealers present, by the pace at which the bids are invited, or by an unworthy fear that discretion may be misinterpreted as meanness or cowardice. There are not as many people who are sublimely indifferent to what their neighbours think as there are those who pretend to be!

A visit to a dealer's gallery may not be as emotionally rousing as a visit to a picture auction, but in the calmer atmosphere that prevails there a collector has a greater chance to consider the price he is being asked to pay for any picture, and is less likely to be rushed into an unpremeditated extravagance.

It must not be too readily believed, though, that the price a picture dealer asks will represent an exact assessment of the market value of any work. There are several other factors involved, besides the age-old counter-tensions of supply and demand. Let us examine—for amusement, possibly, as well as instruction—the hypothetical case of an imaginary artist called X, whose pictures can be viewed and purchased at a small, luxuriously appointed gallery not far from Bond Street, London (or 57th Street or Madison Avenue, New York, or the Champs-Elysées in Paris—the address is immaterial: the methods of the international art trade are not much affected by frontiers). How did his pictures get there? Who fixed the price asked for each in the typewritten list pinned up by the door?

To begin with, X has an unrewarding struggle for recognition that lasts for several years. During that time he paints scores of attractive pictures and sends several of the best of them to mixed exhibitions, where, unfortunately for X and for Mrs X (who is helping to support her husband by doing a little part-time teaching) and for the little Xes (who have no nice expensive toys, like the children of successful painters) these pictures have to compete for the attention of the buying public with the works of hundreds of other artists, who are as avid for fame and fortune and for the home comforts that prosperity can bring as Mr and Mrs X, and they return from the exhibitions unsold. 'Why don't you show your pictures to some of the *dealers*, dear?' Mrs X asks occasionally, more in sorrow than in earnest, and X dutifully sets off for a currently fashionable gallery with a bundle of unframed canvases under his arm. His journeys are always in vain, though. Few of the fashionable proprietors even trouble to make a note of his name.

At last, by an unpredictable turn of fortune's wheel, X gets his chance when a young dealer who is not yet quite in the top flight takes a fancy to his work and offers him an agreement. The terms of these contracts vary from dealer to dealer. In the case of X, the agreement is to last for two years, the main clauses stipulating that the artist shall deliver a certain number of approved canvases in the first period of twelve months, and a comparable number in the second year. As recompense, the dealer agrees to pay X a small sum every month, which is rather less than he would get if he were clearing snow off the streets for the Borough Council. The Xes are not aggrieved—they are overjoyed. At least X's paintings will be publicly exhibited at somebody else's expense, and may even be sold, instead of gathering dust and taking up valuable house room.

A month or two later, X's first one-man show is announced, to take place at the dealer's softly carpeted gallery. This, for the dealer, is rather in the nature of a hazard, for the cost of printing and sending out invitations to all the clients and critics on his mailing list, advertising, and, possibly, providing liquid refreshments for the private view will mount up to quite a sum.

To get this sum back, plus the stipend he is paying to X, plus a reasonable margin of profit, the dealer has to use all his skill and judgement in compiling the price list. Possibly, he will discuss the matter with X, to save X's feelings, but X, in making the agreement, will almost certainly have signed away temporarily all the rights he ever had to trade in his own work, so his views will be listened to solely out of courtesy. The prices in the catalogue will not be high, though, you can be sure of that. Not for the work of an unknown artist.

The day of the private view is, possibly, one of the most crucial in X's life. For a few hours, he is surrounded by over-confident people, most of whom he has never seen before, many of them saying things about his pictures that he is unable to understand. When these people go, there will be, if he is lucky, small red spots on the corners of at least one-third of the pictures, to show that they have found purchasers. If the dealer has earned a good reputation for adding winners to his 'stable' the proportion of pictures sold will probably be higher than that.

Next day, a new price list will almost certainly take the place of the tentative catalogue that served for the private view. In the revised list, each of the unsold pictures will be marked up by a few pounds, and the prices may be increased again in the following few days if the critics' reviews of the exhibition are favourable. There will be a further factor operating on X's behalf, too—the people who have bought his paintings will be talking about them to their friends. This acts as free publicity, and it will be still more effective when the paintings are taken away at the close of the exhibition.

The next few months are for X a period of steady consolidation. During this time, he works, if he is wise, with more vigour than he has ever worked before. His dealer will be working on X's behalf, too—mentioning his name in articles he writes for the press, nominating his paintings for 'prestige' exhibitions abroad, inviting him to meet prominent compilers of gossip columns—the tracks followed in this particular rat race are well worn. Even Mrs X may be helping to further her husband's career, at this stage. On the days when she is not teaching she will probably visit the private views of Y and Z, to make remarks about their paintings that they, too, are unable to understand.

So, it would seem advisable for you—if you are going to regard your collection of pictures as a form of investment, hoping for capital gain—to look out for, and buy, the works of artists like X *before* they have started to rise. That is easier said than done, of course, but it is not impossible. Several of the painters whose names are now internationally known have spent years of their lives hawking their pictures round Paris cafés with little or no success. Maurice Utrillo and Raoul Dufy (to name only two examples) were tragically under-appreciated until they had competent dealers to take charge of their affairs. If you do find a young unknown artist whose outlook appeals to you, and if you add one or more of his works to your collection, you will not be gambling on a fortuitous dice-throw, you will be backing the soundness of your own judgement. You may never see your stake again, but it will have gone in a good cause, and if you have chosen wisely your little flutter will yield you a lot of pleasure and excitement.

And if you happen to have bestowed your patronage on the right man—on a worthy but under-estimated fellow like X, say, who is just on the eve of popular acclaim? Then, your investment may yield you much more than that. The capital you have laid out may be doubled or trebled, almost overnight. You will be able to realize your capital, too, with its added profit, almost as soon as you want it—as long as you keep one step ahead of the moves in the market. For the prices of modern pictures can fluctuate almost as unpredictably as the prices of industrial equities. Let us look, for a salutary warning, at the further adventures of X.

We left him, you will remember, with his name being bandied about as one of the coming young men. Unfortunately, one can only go on being a coming young man for a certain length of time before one is in danger of becoming a has-been. Less than a year after X's work hits the headlines for the first time, some of his early paintings come on to the open market when the percipient people who bought them in the lean days, before he was discovered, decide to take their profit. Unless X's dealer is in a position to influence the price at which they change hands (it is not unknown for such a man to 'buy in' the works of the artists in his stable, under some cover that will effectively conceal his identity) they may not reach the carefully inflated levels that prevail in their home gallery. This is bound to put a brake on the rising spiral, at least temporarily, if it does not actually cause the bubble to burst.

As the date approaches when his original agreement with his dealer will cease to be valid, X faces further tests of strength—he may not be offered an extension on agreeable terms. Alternatively, he may not be offered an extension at all. Worse, he may be offered seductive contracts by competing dealers who may try to persuade him to change his style, or to limit his output so that he lessens the risk of flooding the market with his work, or to comply in any one of a dozen ways with ideas that are, to say the least of it, non-creative. X may survive these tests, but he will need to be a person of real integrity if he is to develop as an artist unscathed.

The work of artists who have been safely dead for a long time is not quite so subject to fluctuation as the work of recently established favourites, as the forces of supply and demand have had a longer time in which to find the right level of equilibrium. If your own nature is in any way conservative, and if your means are limited, you will probably prefer to collect pictures by artists who are 'known' without being famous, which have a steady market value, since, with them, you will know more or less exactly where you are. That does not mean to say that a collection of pictures of this sort need be lacking in distinction, or that it will not be as covetable as the collections made by your more daring friends. What could be more delightful, as an integral part of your normal home surroundings, than a group of portrait miniatures, pleasantly displayed, or a collection of silhouettes?

Portrait miniatures have been popular in England ever since the days when Nicholas Hilliard (1537–1619) and his pupil Isaac Oliver first recorded the features of their royal sitters on the tiniest possible scale and, at the behest of Queen Elizabeth I, without the unflattering use of shadows to suggest relief. Some of the most prolific painters of miniatures have been comparatively celebrated artists, and examples of their work tend to be expensive (you will be lucky if you find a genuine miniature by Richard Cosway, Samuel Cooper or John Smart at less than £20), but it is not difficult to find miniatures by lesser men which are quite charming, and contain just as much carefully observed detail as most life-size portraits on canvas.

If you decide to collect portrait miniatures, you will probably be offered examples of three different kinds.

First, there are the miniatures painted in water-colours that were produced in enormous quantities in the last decades of the eighteenth century. Many of these were painted on ivory, which tends to warp if it is hung or stored in an excessively dry place. Others were painted on paper or vellum.

On the Dogger Bank, painted by Clarkson Stanfield, ʀ.ᴀ. (1793–1867). Many Victorian paintings as graphic as this can still be found in shops that sell second-hand goods

Bulls Fighting; St Donatt's Castle in the Distance: James Ward, R.A. (1769–1859). If you find any pictures that resemble this, you may have discovered some of the 'missing' Wards

All should be protected from the direct rays of the sun, or their colours will fade.

Then there are the miniatures painted with oil-colours by artists accustomed to working in the more robust medium. Sometimes these would be produced as 'consolation prizes' for those people (usually, the cadet members of a family) who were not entitled to receive a replica of a full-size portrait.

The most unusual miniatures are those painted with enamel colours. This technique was one extraordinarily difficult to learn and to practise consistently, since the colours had to be 'fixed' by being fired in a furnace, during which process their appearance would change out of all recognition. A portrait painter wishing to represent the delicate rosy pink of a young lady's cheek, for instance, might have to stipple it in with a mud-like patina of grey or brown metallic oxide. The effort all this involved was considerable, but it may be thought to have been worth while, for true enamel portrait miniatures, properly carried out on a copper base, are virtually indestructible.

A collection of silhouettes can be just as interesting as a collection of portrait miniatures, in spite of the fact that the 'colour element' will almost inevitably be missing. It is amazing how much can be suggested by a small scrap of black paper that has been trimmed into significance at the hands of a master cutter.

One of the earliest of these virtuosi was Jean Huber (1722–1790). 'Who has not heard of Huber?' asks a M. Desnoires-terres. 'Of his vivid, fine cuttings-out, free and flowing as pencil drawings, reproducing every object with an arresting truth?' Probably few people today will have heard of Huber, though his varied talents made him famous enough in his time. 'Huber will paint you in pastel, in oil, *ex-mezzo-tinto*,' wrote Voltaire to Mme du Deffand in August 1779. 'He will cut you out on a card with scissors, all in caricature, and he has made me thus ridiculous from one end of Europe to the other.' Voltaire was at first a great admirer of Huber's skill, allowing him to run in and out of his house at all times of the day and night until he eventually became rather tired of being 'cut out' under the most ludicrous and embarrassing

4

conditions. Grimm refers to the cut-outs in his correspondence, and he sent some to Berlin and others to Gotha.

But Huber was never satisfied with his own achievements. '[He] is, moreover, ceaselessly perfecting his processes,' wrote one of his contemporaries, a M. Baud-Bovy. 'For the scissors he substitutes a fine, keen blade, and for paper, vellum. He goes so far as to employ in the same picture transparent vellums of different colours, and to model with his point on the surface of the fragile skin the leaves of the trees.' De Goncourt wrote of 'this art, which produced its great genius in the great Huber—the Watteau, the Callot and the Paul Potter of inspired cutting-out.'

Of especial interest to the members of the medical profession are many of the silhouettes cut by Augustin Edouart (active *c.* 1825), who made a good living touring the provinces to carry out commissions, and at one time was able to employ a number of assistants. For some reason, a high proportion of Edouart's patrons were medical men.

Edouart was not slow, though, to turn his attention to any subject that might have a more popular appeal. When an old pensioner died at an Edinburgh lodging-house, early in the nineteenth century, William Hare, who kept the house, and William Burke, who was a guest there, sold the dead body to Dr Knox, the great anatomist, for £7 10*s*. Hare then seems to have suggested that it would be a profitable business to attract unknown wayfarers to the lodging-house and kill them, afterwards selling the bodies to those who were too discreet to ask any questions. The wives of Burke and Hare almost certainly assisted in this macabre traffic, and within a few months at least fifteen bodies had been delivered and satisfactorily paid for.

The methods used by Burke and Hare were singularly tactful—they made their victims drunk and then suffocated them gently, so that no marks of violence would be visible on the traded cadavers. When Burke was tried in the High Court of Judiciary in Edinburgh in 1829—Hare turned King's Evidence—Edouart was busily at work, and his studies of the accused, the court officials, the counsel involved, and the members of the jury are cut with inimitable skill.

And what is the origin of the word 'silhouette'? It was not, as many people think, derived from the name of the man who first cut profile portraits out of black paper with scissors, but from one Étienne de Silhouette, who was born at Limoges in 1709, and who became, later, councillor to the *parlement* of Metz, secretary to the Duke of Orleans, member of the commission set up to de-limit Franco-British interests in Acadia, royal commissioner in the Indies Company, and, finally, Controller-General of France. When he took office in his last

13.   A silhouette of Dr Bougon, cut by
Augustin Edouart, 1830

and most illustrious appointment, de Silhouette had the complete confidence of the Court and the nobility, but his financial measures proved disastrous, and he was driven from office in less than a year. The people who had lost so much of their wealth and possessions through his ineptitude were ready enough to apply his name to a flimsy figure reduced to its simplest possible form.

It is virtually certain that miniature portraits and silhouettes will be sufficiently unusual subjects to satisfy the most unorthodox collector, but there are other kinds of reasonably-priced treasures which have an appeal that is even more esoteric. Collections could be formed (to take only three examples) of the three-dimensional 'ship' pictures made usually by landed or retired mariners in the nineteenth century, of pictures made from shells and seaweed, and of early group photographs. These can all be classified loosely as pictures, if they are not exactly works of art! One day, they will probably be highly valued.

5

COLLECTING OIL-PAINTINGS

NOBODY knows who invented oil-colours, but it seems likely that the Flemish brothers Hubert and Jan Van Eyck played a big part in their development during the early years of the fifteenth century, and it is possible that they were introduced into Italy a little later by an artist called Antonello da Messina. We do know for certain that they immediately became enormously popular with artists throughout the Western world, and rendered virtually obsolete the tempera and fresco techniques favoured by the artists we now tend to think of as 'primitives'.

You will certainly understand why oil-colours came into favour so rapidly, and why they have remained so popular for four and a half centuries, if you have ever done any oil painting yourself. The luscious consistency of the colours—they feel like fat or butter on the brush—the richness of the hues that can be obtained when suitable pigments are combined with oils or essences, and the subtle gradations that result when one oily shade or tint is merged almost imperceptibly with another—all these give a special pleasure that may never be known by the practitioners of less flexible kinds of painting. You can get that pleasure vicariously, if you are completely devoid of artistic talent, by collecting oil-paintings and by studying their paint surfaces with especial care.

One of the first things you will notice when you examine an oil-painting closely is the wide variety of textures produced as the colours are applied to the 'support'. Oil-paints can be built up into lumps and ridges of thick opaque 'impasto' if the artist wishes, so that the mouth will positively water at their creamy sensuousness. Alternatively, they can be applied in the thinnest of transparent or translucent films or 'glazes', or dragged lightly with a dry brush over an existing paint surface to provide a delicate 'scumble'. Connoisseurs look for and appreciate these first-hand traces of an artist's prowess, finding in them a source of enjoyment that can never be satisfactorily provided by a reproduction, however faithful a facsimile this may be.

Normally, any oil-painting you are offered will consist of three intimately connected parts—the support, mentioned above; the tough leathery film or skin of paint that conveys the artist's message; and the 'ground' that separates these two. As the value of any oil-painting you may add to your collection will depend on the condition of all three of these factors, let us examine them, briefly, in turn.

Canvases are traditionally the favourite supports of artists painting in oils, but other bases have been becoming steadily more popular in recent years, and many modern painters do not use canvases at all.

'Canvas' is a term used loosely to describe a number of different woven materials that can be fastened over a 'stretcher' (this word is explained below) or applied with glue or some other adhesive to a rigid panel. Some cloths are affected noticeably by changes in atmospheric conditions, others are comparatively inert. If differences in humidity make the fibres of a fabric shrink and stretch to an abnormal degree, the grounds and paints applied to that fabric will tend to deteriorate rapidly—cracks may appear in the surface of a painting, and parts of a favourite work may even peel right off. Fortunately, it is possible to have such a picture 're-lined' by a professional restorer. This operation, which is rather expensive, is described in Chapter 11. It is advisable, obviously, to hang oil-paintings where they will not be subjected to any extremes.

'Stretchers' are tongued and grooved wooden frames on which a fabric can be kept taut. Most stretchers are provided with triangular wooden pegs or wedges which can be driven in between the members if atmospheric conditions or the passage of time make the fabric floppy.

If you are unlucky enough to pick up a desirable canvas that is tacked down over a rigid and immovable wooden frame, you may be able to re-stretch the canvas by removing the original tacks carefully with a pair of pincers. You can make the canvas taut again more or less satisfactorily with your fingers alone, but you will probably make a better job of it if you invest a few shillings in a pair of straining pliers like those shown in Fig. 14. Use galvanized tacks as replacements, if you can obtain some. Ordinary flat-headed domestic tacks (known to artists as 'canvas tacks') are almost as good, but they have a slight tendency to rust with the passage of time.

You will find it easiest to re-stretch a canvas if you start with the tacks at the middle of each side, working, afterwards, outwards towards the corners. The canvas has to be pulled as tight as possible before each tack is driven home.

14. Straining pliers

If you buy an oil-painting that has been applied more or less directly to a wooden panel, you will not have to worry about tacking or stretching, but that does not mean to say that you will be entirely free from trouble. Rubens's great landscape *The Château de Steen* developed a horrifying fissure during the severe winter of 1946–7 when the National Gallery was insufficiently heated!

Very few supports can be used without some special preparation that will make them less absorbent, more suitable in tone as a basis for a painting, more suitable in colour, more suitable in texture, or any combination of those four.

A 'priming' is a preparation, usually liquid, that makes a surface a little less like blotting-paper. An unprimed canvas will soak up the oil from any paints that are put on it until they look meagre and floury. The oil makes the canvas rot quickly, the painting deteriorates, nobody is happy except the picture restorers. Usually you will be able to take it for granted that any painting you are offered will be on a surface that has been satisfactorily primed, but just occasionally you may notice signs of 'starvation'.

A 'ground' consists of an opaque substance such as slaked plaster, whiting (calcium carbonate), or white lead powder, made up in a suitably retentive liquid or mixture of liquids. Usually, this will be visible wherever it has not been completely covered by the oil paint film. It may repay close inspection, since many painters like to paint on grounds which have had some colour added, to give a warm or cool tone to the underlying surfaces of the picture—Constable's atmospheric landscape sketches, many of which were painted on chestnut-coloured grounds, are examples which spring at once to the mind. Coloured or toned grounds would be entirely admirable if oil-colours did not tend to become slightly more transparent with the passage of time. As it is, they often have a darkening effect, and pictures painted on them rarely retain the same sparkle as those painted on a pure brilliant white surface.

Knowing this, some of the members of the Pre-Raphaelite Brotherhood evolved a distinctive technique. Before starting work, they would spread a layer of fresh white oil-paint on part of their canvas, and then they would lay the colours on this with very soft fine brushes, working so delicately that the wet undercoat was not disturbed. At its best (as, for example, in Millais's *Ophelia*, now in the Tate Gallery) this difficult technique produced a brilliant, gem-like surface, but unfortunately the members of the Brotherhood did not number a good colour sense among their many assets, and most of their paintings demonstrate the dangers of working with an unlimited palette.

Most members of the lay public who think about pictures at all believe that all oil-paintings are the better, when finished, for a good coat of varnish. This is only partly true, as varnish can do irremediable damage if it is used without discrimination. Here are some points to remember when you examine the superficial surface of any oil-painting:

Varnish is used to protect the surface of a painting from the harmful effects of moisture, gases and dirt in the atmosphere.

It seems to give the colours of a painting greater brilliance and luminosity.

It can be used to give the surface of a picture a uniformly shiny, semi-shiny or matt finish, according to the kind of varnish chosen.

Against those benefits can be set two distinct drawbacks:

A coat of varnish which becomes discoloured or dirty can only be removed at the risk of a certain amount of damage to the paint surface. If copal varnish is used, it is virtually impossible to remove without causing a certain amount of deterioration.

A varnished painting is liable to suffer from 'bloom' or mistiness if it is exposed to damp, or if the varnish has not been applied under the best possible conditions. You can read more about this in Chapter 11.

Most of the oil-paintings you acquire will have been painted for so long that the paint will have had a chance to dry out thoroughly, and the question of whether to varnish or not will have been settled for you already by the artist, or by some previous owner. Should a recently completed but unvarnished picture come into your possession, don't rush to varnish it without giving the matter a great deal of thought.

The word 'dry' is rather misleading when applied to the hardening of oil-paints. What is really happening is much more complex. Parts of the oil in which the pigment is ground oxidize slowly, drawing oxygen from the atmosphere as they do so, and forming a tough, leathery skin. The outside hardens first, of course, as it is in direct contact with the air. As more oil oxidizes, gases are given off that make tiny holes and channels in the skin already formed. If you put a coat of varnish on a picture that has been painted for less than a year you may be sealing off a surface that is still as active as the crater of a volcano.

There is, however, a substance known as 'Retouching

Varnish' that can be applied safely to the surface of a picture almost as soon as the paint is firm enough to take it. Retouching varnish is not as substantial as copal varnish or mastic varnish and it is not suitable for use as a permanent protective covering, but you may find it useful as a temporary expedient for bringing up any part of a new picture that has gone rather 'flat', or dry and lifeless.

Obviously, oil-paintings that have been built up with a thick impasto will present more technical difficulties than pictures in which the artist has used only a very thin skin of paint. A fat gobbet of colour half an inch or so thick may be a very stimulating thing to look at, especially if it has been applied to the support in such a way that it shows the brushwork (or the trowelwork) of a master, but it will be a potential source of trouble for quite as long as it has a liquid and chemically active core, and possibly longer. Vincent Van Gogh and a few other artists who have wished to exploit the emotive quality of a heavily built-up paint surface have experimented with wax mediums of various kinds, but none can be certified to be completely satisfactory over a period of years. It is tempting to add a number of bold, exuberant 'palette knife' paintings to a collection, but one has to remember the undoubted tendency of works of this kind to crack and flake, and their tendency, too, to harbour dust in the interstices in the loaded pigment.

It is not surprising that oil paintings tend to predominate in the majority of collections of pictures, since oil-colours are capable of being used in so many different ways, to suit the individual needs of so many artists. As a collector, you may find a comparative study of the most commonly used techniques particularly rewarding, since it will help you to appreciate the full beauties of this infinitely flexible medium, and it may help you, too, to assign some of your 'doubtful' accessions to their correct periods in the history of art, without the possibly expensive advice of an expert.

First, you may find it useful to examine closely an uncompleted painting from a comparatively early period—there are instructive examples by several Renaissance painters in the National Gallery, London, if you can get there.

For a work of this sort, which would be built up in easy stages over a comparatively protracted period, the artist would usually prepare a 'cartoon' or preliminary drawing, that would be exactly the same size as the support.

Then he would transfer the outlines to the ground by one of several alternative methods. One of the easiest processes would require the use of a needle. With this, the artist (or one of his assistants) would prick holes all along the lines to be transferred. Then, having fixed the cartoon over the canvas or panel he would pounce powdered charcoal over the paper so that some of the fine grey dust would pass through the holes. This would leave a number of tiny dark spots on the smooth white ground. It would be a comparatively easy matter to join these spots up so that they became continuous lines, thus reproducing exactly the outlines of the cartoon.

Next the artist, guided by these outlines, would lay in the shadows and the half-tones of his picture, using a paint made from 'terre verte' (a lovely soft green earth) or some similar fairly neutral monochrome. He would carefully avoid covering any part of the ground if he intended that part to be light when the picture was finished. It was clearly desirable to leave the white ground to go on providing its original brilliance for as long as possible.

Several weeks—or, possibly, months—might be allowed to pass before further coats of paint were added to the picture. Then the artist would superimpose on his monochromatic underpainting a succession of transparent and semi-transparent glazes, each of which would add some local colour or reinforce the modelling. Where terre verte had been used for the underpainting, the addition of some warm pinks would produce the colour of flesh in a particularly subtle and beautiful way. This technical device can be seen clearly in the partly completed *Entombment* by Michelangelo in the National Gallery, London.

The technique of covering an underpainting with a succession of glazes was carried to the ultimate in careful perfection by the Venetian painters of the sixteenth century. Titian, Tintoretto, Veronese and several of their contemporaries produced many masterpieces in which the shades and tints glow like the colours of the richest stained glass. It would never have been possible to produce a blue as enchanting and as mysterious as the background of Titian's *Portrait of a Man in Blue* (in the National Gallery, London) just by grinding up a single pigment, mixing it with a suitable binding medium, and applying it to a canvas. Even real ultramarine, which is made by powdering the semi-precious stone lapis lazuli, seems relatively strident if it is used without any ancillary glaze. This is how one contemporary described the technique of Richard Wilson:

'Wilson dead-coloured in a very broad, simple manner, giving a faint idea of the effect and colour intended, but without any strong dark, quite flat, and no handling whatever; the shadows in the foreground thin and clear; air tint prevailing.

'When perfectly dry, he went over it a second time, heightening every part with colour, and deepening the shadows, but still brown, free, loose and flat, and left in a state for finishing, the half tints laid in, without high lights. The third time he altered what was necessary in the masses of tint, adding all the necessary sharpness and handling to the different objects, and then gave the finish to his picture.

'His great care was to bring up all the parts of his picture together, and not to finish one part before another, so that the picture should not, as the painters term it, run away with him, and that while working in one part he should introduce that colour into the other parts where it suited, or to lower the tone fit to make it suit, that the different parts might keep company with each other.

'His air tint was blue, burnt ochre, and light red, sometimes a little vermilion, and, in other cases, he made his air tint of the lakes and blue; with the lakes he made his glazing tints on the foreground very rich and warm, and of their full force; but all this was moderated by the tints which he laid on the glazings. If any part was hard he restored it by scumbling the air tint, suited to the distance of the part, over it, and then added the finishing touches and sharpness, to prevent its being smoky or mealy. A maglyph or majellup, of linseed oil and mastic varnish, in which the latter predominated, was his usual vehicle, and an oyster shell served him to contain it. He dead-coloured with Prussian blue, but always finished the sky and distance with ultramarine for it was his opinion that no other blue could give the beautiful effect of air.'

Paul Sandby, who was an intimate friend of Wilson's—he is said to have hawked many of Wilson's paintings around when the great man was in low water, purchasing them himself, under assumed names, when he failed to find any customers—has left us a slightly different version of Wilson's methods. It is quite probable, though, that Wilson used two different techniques, each of them appropriate to a different type of picture. Rubens is a particularly good example of an artist who was always ready to vary his methods. In his case, the colour chosen for the basic work was often grey, with warmer additions of rich reddish-brown in the really deep shadows.

The paintings of Thomas Gainsborough offer a refreshing contrast to more ponderous works, produced with majestic deliberation. Gainsborough enjoyed using his paint in very thin washes, diluting them liberally with turpentine so that occasionally they dripped off his palette on to the floor. The dry, floury look of Gainsborough's paintings is largely due to the low content of oil in the paint film. It is doubtful whether Gainsborough could have produced pictures of such extraordinary delicacy if he had used a more orthodox and heavier technique.

Later painters have tended to discard the slow, methodical techniques of the early masters altogether, preferring to paint directly, with the majority of their colours mixed up and applied to the canvas at a single sitting instead of being built up in thin coats over a period of many weeks. These more hurried methods may give a greater appearance of spontaneity to a picture, but they do not make for greater permanence or for the incomparable richness of the finest Renaissance canvases.

As you study the history and development of oil-painting you may get some special pleasure from the work of certain idiosyncratic artists who have exploited the resources of the medium in an unusual or even peculiar way.

You may enjoy looking at the small panels of Samuel Palmer (1805–1881) for instance. Palmer was a real romantic who referred to himself once, in a moment of self-truth, as a 'pure, quaint, crinkle-crankle Goth'. A member of a strange band of young men who called themselves 'The Ancients', he combed Sussex for forgotten traces of a vanished world, for obscure corners where ruined barns, riven tree trunks, weedy pools and overgrown copses brought a strong nostalgic flavour of the primeval world into the trim pictures of the nineteenth century. But Palmer did not react only to the decaying and bizarre. Many of his small landscapes—of blossoming orchards, of shady elm clumps and of moonlit harvest fields—are pastoral poems as charming as any that have ever been written with words, and you will be lucky if you get the chance to possess one.

Walter Richard Sickert (1860–1942) is another artist whose works have an unusual flavour many people appreciate. Sickert was associated in his early days with the great actor-manager Sir Henry Irving, and there is an obvious theatricality about his paintings of faded music halls and tawdry lodging-houses that makes them immediately compelling. He was strongly influenced in his youth by Edgar Degas, and as he was one of the first painters to work directly from squared-up newspaper photographs he may fairly be called one of the initiators of Pop Art.

As well as studying the works of individual artists, you may like to do a bit of research into the origins and development of certain unusual oil-paint techniques that are especially interesting from a collector's point of view. For example, you might enjoy making a study of 'pointillisme', that laborious method of building up a paint surface devised by Georges Seurat (1859–1891) and perfected by his disciple Paul Signac, in which tiny spots of pure or almost pure colour were intimately combined on the canvas without being mixed together. It would be difficult to imagine a painting technique that differed more completely from the fluid vaporizings and washings-in of Gainsborough, but this versatility is, as was stressed earlier, one of the principal advantages of oil-colours and makes a collection of oil-paintings an inexhaustible source of interest to the connoisseur.

It has been pointed out already that oil-colours tend with the passage of time to become more transparent. It follows, therefore, that any oil-painting that has been subjected to a certain amount of alteration will be liable, after the lapse of some years, to produce 'pentimenti' or unwanted images, unless the artist has been careful to scrape away every trace of the work he has wished to amend—covering it with further coats of paint is much too chancy. It is amusing, rather than annoying, to find examples of these unpremeditated re-appearances in a collection—in the Prado, for instance, there is a horse painted by Velasquez in the seventeenth century that has, by the twentieth, 'grown' two extra legs!

6

COLLECTING WATER-COLOURS

IF OIL-COLOURS are essentially masculine and vigorous, water-colours are reticent, restrained and feminine. That does not mean that either medium will appeal more to male picture collectors, or to the female of the species, but it may explain why so many buyers will have a marked preference for one type of picture, virtually to the exclusion of the other. Water-colours may even seem meagre and lifeless to people who admire—say—the slightly florid canvases of Sir Matthew Smith.

The difference between the two kinds of painting is fundamental. In oil-painting, opaque colours can be used freely, as their visual message will be carried by the light reflected from their outer surfaces. In water-colour painting, the colours used must be transparent, or nearly so, as they will depend for their value on the light that is reflected from the paper to which they have been applied.

Strictly interpreted, water-colour painting is not a very ancient technique. It was developed in England and has always appealed more strongly to artists working in England than to artists working in other countries—unkind critics have ascribed this to the wateriness of the British climate. In France, true water-colour painting is sometimes referred to as the 'English method', French artists preferring 'gouache', in which they may add white body colour. This, of course, makes the colours opaque.

It follows, then, that only the finest and most luminous papers can be used for true water-colour painting, and it follows, too, that the purest pigments have to be applied to them with the softest of brushes in the thinnest of washes. It is not possible, or desirable, to build up a water-colour impasto.

Here are some of the considerations that have to be borne in mind by the artist when he obtains his equipment for this difficult technique. It is impossible to produce water-colour pictures of lasting quality with any but the choicest materials.

The best papers for water-colour painting are undoubtedly those that have been specially prepared for the purpose, and the most desirable of these are the grades that have had only the best linen rags used in their manufacture. If these have been bleached by the action of water and sun without any assistance from chemicals they are sure to be very expensive.

A little cheaper, and nearly as satisfying to paint on and to look at, are the papers that contain an admixture of cotton rag. A long way behind come the ordinary papers that are made with wood pulp. These will probably have been bleached with chlorine, dressed with china clay or gypsum, given false brilliance with the old blue bag, and treated in so many other ways that they are most unsuitable for use with a delicate medium.

Paper that has been well prepared will last for hundreds of years: cheap paper may deteriorate in a matter of months: anyone who intends to collect water-colour paintings seriously should learn to tell the difference between the two by examining closely (and touching) examples of each.

Normally, an artist will 'stretch' a piece of paper before he starts to paint on it with water-colours. To do this, he first damps it thoroughly and then he puts it in a special frame like that used by embroiderers or he fixes it to a drawing-board or some similar flat surface by sticking adhesive strip round its edges. When the paper has dried out it will be as taut as the skin of a drum, and it will retain this splendidly level quality long after it has been cut away from its temporary base and framed. A water-colour that has been carried out on unstretched paper or, worse, on one of the sketching-blocks made up specially for amateurs may soon curve or belly in an unsightly way.

A few artists have liked to work in water-colours on damp paper. It is usually fairly easy to tell by the softness and lack of precise definition of the forms when this technique has been used.

5

The brushes normally used for water-colour painting are made from squirrel (or Kolinsky) tails, and are known in the trade as 'sables'. These are ideal for applying the diluted colour to the paper in large or small patches of smooth, even tone.

Gum arabic is the agent traditionally used to bind the pigments in water-colour painting, but nowadays, with this gum in short supply, African gums are usually substituted, and synthetic materials are used by some manufacturers. Water-colour paints are marketed in two different ways—as dry blocks, or moist in collapsible tubes like small toothpaste containers. As there is a tendency for colours packed in tubes to dry out and become hard, they are usually given a small admixture of honey, glycerine or sugar to keep them workable. Pictures painted with sweetened colours have been known to attract flies, and as these persistent little creatures are no respecters of any picture surface it is a good idea—if for no other reason—to keep valuable water-colour paintings behind glass.

Unfortunately, water-colour paints are not always as permanent as they might be—pigments in gum being noticeably less well protected from the harmful effects of the atmosphere than the same pigments ground in oil. French blue or artificial ultramarine is one notable example (in oil, this useful colour rarely fades so perceptibly that it defeats the artist's intentions unless it is actually mixed with lead white). Prussian blue may fade when it is exposed to light, but it is said to recover its intensity when stored in the dark!

There is a tendency, too, for many yellow pigments used as water-colours to be affected by damp. Paper is notoriously absorbent, and as the humidity of the atmosphere changes, so does the moisture content of the paper. The damage that may be caused by this may be minimized if pictures are hung in a room that is kept at an even, moderate temperature with adequate but not excessive ventilation. If you see moisture condensing on the inside of the glass over a framed water-colour, the conditions are definitely not suitable for it.

With a sheet of stretched Whatman, Arnold or Michellet paper, a suitable sable brush and some diluted water-colours, an experienced artist can produce a painted surface that has a very unusual and specially beautiful quality. This will almost certainly involve the delicate operation known as 'laying a wash' (or a series of washes) for the manner in which a water-colour painter applies his paint to the paper surface will help to determine the ultimate value of his work. An even film of paint that is allowed to dry without being re-worked or stippled or cross-hatched or messed about with in any way will have a 'bloom' not unlike that on the petals of a freshly opened flower, or a grape that has never been touched.

Collectors of water-colour paintings have a more restricted field for their activities than print collectors, or collectors of oil-paintings, because the number of artists who have mastered the technical difficulties of the medium is relatively limited. Here is a brief review of some of the outstanding figures in the history of art who have used water-colours as their main medium of expression, and not just as some conveniently portable sketching apparatus.

Alexander Cozens (died 1786) was a painter of poetical landscapes, choosing for his subjects rocky mountains, wooded valleys and great formations of dark and threatening clouds. He was said to have been a natural son of Peter the Great and an Englishwoman from Deptford. He studied art in Italy and did not come to England until 1746. Between the years 1763 and 1768 he was drawing master at Eton, and he published a number of treatises on art. One of the ways in which he encouraged his students to begin work is worthy of notice—he would flick a pen charged with ink at the piece of paper on which he intended to make a picture, and he would use the ink splashes thus fortuitously obtained as a basis for his composition. Eventually, he is said to have been given the nickname 'Blotmaster to the Town'.

Cozens's son John Robert was born in London in 1752, and he was brought up with a family background that must have been extremely stimulating to a potential painter. His water-colour sketches were usually in monochrome, and he became quite adept at suggesting delicate atmospheric effects with a few carefully placed washes of tone. He was, in one sense, quite a revolutionary, since he ignored all the classical laws of pictorial composition by which most of his contemporaries considered themselves bound. Orthodoxy may be thought to have triumphed in the end, however, for the younger Cozens spent the last years of his life in a lunatic asylum.

Let us look, in passing, at a small group of minor English artists who were all born a few years before the brilliant young Cozens, but who were fortunate enough to survive him. Each, painting for the most part in water-colours, managed to combine in his own way some fashionable elements of the 'picturesque' or 'sublime' with the carefully delineated topographical details that are always popular. Every one may be said to have played some small part in preparing for the considerable achievements of the undoubtedly more original artists who were born towards the end of the century.

First of this rather arbitrarily selected group came Francis Towne (1740–1816). Towne was born in Devon, but he did most of his work in the mountainous districts of Wales, Italy and Switzerland. His paintings of peaks, crags and torrents have a quiet authority which is the direct result of Towne's profound and scientific study of geology, but you will be extremely lucky if you are able to add an original example to your collection, for his output was relatively limited.

Thomas Hearne (1744–1817) was born near Malmesbury in Wiltshire. He was apprenticed to William Wollett the engraver, with whom he stayed for six years. In 1771, Hearne went to the Leeward Islands with Lord Lavington, the recently appointed Governor, and stayed there for three and a half years, making drawings of many of the most notable features of the islands. This survey, and the further work he did on his return, turned Hearne's interests from engraving to the speedier techniques of water-colour painting, and his studies for *The Antiquities of Great Britain*, made during several extensive tours, did a lot to draw public attention to his country's extraordinarily fine architectural heritage.

Michael Rooker (1745–1801) was taught engraving by his father Edward Rooker and drawing by Paul Sandby at the

St Martin's Lane School and at the Royal Academy. Rooker is usually referred to as 'Michael Angelo Rooker', having been given this name by his master Sandby as a passing jest (as so often happens, the name stuck). Best known for the charming studies of architectural remains that he brought back from his annual autumnal tours in the country, Rooker is also remembered as the chief scene painter at the Haymarket Theatre, where he appeared in the playbills as 'Signor Rookerini'.

Thomas Malton (1748–1804) was a most conscientious and accomplished architectural draughtsman. His views of London streets and buildings earned him much popularity, and he received a gold medal from the Academy and a premium from the Society of Arts. His works are still consulted by students who need access to authentic portrayals of the eighteenth-century scene, and he is best known perhaps for his monumental publication *A Picturesque Tour through the Cities of London and Westminster* which he illustrated with a hundred aquatint plates.

Greater by far than any of these charming minor artists were two men who were born in the same momentous year, 1775, and who were both received as pupils by Thomas Malton.

Let us consider Thomas Girtin first, for he crammed into the years of his youth so much feverish activity that he seems to have burned himself out at the comparatively tender age of twenty-seven. 'If Girtin had lived, I should have starved,' Turner is reputed to have said. That may or may not be true, but it is certain that both artistically and technically Girtin was a great innovator. In his formative years, Girtin worked in the traditional manner—that is, he would start each picture by laying in a series of monochrome washes, adding local colours only when the 'light and shade' had been positively established with a carefully modulated foundation of tone. In his later work, Girtin tried to paint more directly, to arrive even at the darkest shadows with a single mixing of pigments. This revolutionary change of method made it possible for him to work at great speed, and it must have released a lot of creative energy, for his landscapes and townscapes had a highly personal quality that made the painstaking studies laboriously built up by his immediate predecessors seem by comparison quite tame and stilted.

Turner's father was a native of Devonshire who had moved up to London and kept a barber's shop at 26 Maiden Lane, Covent Garden. The boy appears to have had the sketchiest of schoolings, and was anything but articulate. By the time he was thirteen he had decided to become an artist. He studied at the Royal Academy Schools and in the house of Sir Joshua Reynolds.

For the first few years of his professional career, Turner worked almost exclusively in water-colour, travelling widely over the British Isles in search of suitable subjects. As quickly as he made his topographical studies, they would be engraved for use as illustrations for Walker's *Copper Plate Magazine* or the *Pocket Magazine*. They showed little originality, and in style were almost indistinguishable from the works of John Robert Cozens, whose sketches Turner had copied, in company with Girtin, at the house of Doctor Munro, an enlightened connoisseur.

With his election to the Associateship of the Royal Academy in 1799, Turner's career entered a new and more adventurous phase. Though still capable of carrying out perspective studies and topographical views 'with a care and completion,' as Ruskin observed, 'which would put the work of any ordinary teacher to utter shame', he allowed the more personal, visionary aspects of picture-making to play an increasing part in his artistic development, 'travelling incessantly', R. H. Wilenski points out, 'because nothing less than experience of the whole world would content him'. Some of the water-colour paintings he made in the last years of his long life are as misty and tenuous as any of the flimsier sketches left by the French Impressionists, but all, however slight, are based on a profound knowledge of geological formations and the experience gained from several decades spent in the most intimate study of nature. When he died he bequeathed nineteen thousand drawings and water-colours and approximately two hundred oil-paintings to the British nation, some of the best of them being permanently on view at the Tate Gallery, London.

Norwich is a place that has been closely associated with water-colour painting ever since a 'school' of artists who were particularly proficient at handling the medium collected in the city and used it as a centre from which to make extremely productive sketching trips into the surrounding country.

John Crome (1768–1821) is usually regarded as the father figure of the Norwich School. Apprenticed as a lad to a coach painter in the city, he was befriended by a wealthy man named Thomas Harvey, who owned pictures by Gainsborough, Richard Wilson, Hobbema and other artists, and who gave Crome some instruction in the elementary processes of drawing and painting. By the time he was thirty-three, Crome had developed his talents so successfully that he was able to form a small art school of his own. He also convened 'The Norwich Society of Artists', an association of the drawing masters and keen amateurs from the locality, who first met to show and discuss their works at a tavern called 'The Hole in the Wall'.

John Sell Cotman (1782–1842) was another Norwich artist associated with the local group whose works, being beautifully designed with broad simple areas of unbroken colour, have a particular appeal today. During the whole of the Victorian era Cotman's paintings were neglected by collectors, and they only started to arouse any great interest in the sale rooms after the taste of the public had veered from the romantic and the sentimental at the close of the century. The works of Crome, Cotman and the other members of the Norwich School can be studied under splendid conditions at the Castle Art Gallery in their native city.

Peter De Wint (1784–1849) was one of the most subtle water-colourists who have ever lived. His father was a doctor who graduated at Leyden, finished his training at St Thomas's Hospital, London, and finally settled down as an apothecary at the little town of Stone, in Staffordshire, where the boy Peter was born.

At an early age, De Wint displayed remarkable artistic talents, and although his parents were agreed that he should enter the medical profession, he managed to persuade his father to apprentice him to the mezzotint engraver John

Raphael Smith. He supplemented the specialized technical instruction he was given in Smith's workrooms by taking a course of general studies at the Royal Academy Schools, and for the rest of his life he managed to make a modest living by painting portraits and landscapes.

Dutch artists have always been fond of choosing as their subjects views of wide stretches of country—usually rather flat, as Holland is—with low horizons and vast expanses of sky. De Wint seems to have inherited or acquired his Dutch ancestors' affection for this type of landscape, and many of the studies he made in Lincolnshire, Cambridgeshire and the neighbouring counties are happily reminiscent of the works of Hobbema, Cuyp and Ruisdael.

After the death of Peter De Wint, water-colour painting in Britain went into decline, and though the medium has been chosen by hundreds of amateur artists of various degrees of competence, few eminent professional artists have used it to produce work of any real distinction. Among the exceptions whose work may interest the serious collector are the members of the Pre-Raphaelite Brotherhood (Dante Gabriel Rossetti's mediaeval romances in water-colour are as rich as stained glass) and, for those who have to limit what they spend on pictures, their numerous associates and followers; Augustus John and J. D. Innes, who reacted romantically to the blue mountains and lakes and the foaming waterfalls of their native Wales; the brothers Nash—the elder, Paul, with his eye for the surrealist qualities of rocks, dead trees and downland, the younger, John, with a wholly delightful feeling for the rich colours and textures of the English countryside; and those two friends with such contrasted personalities Walter Richard Sickert and Philip Wilson Steer (1860–1942). Sickert has been mentioned already in Chapter 5; Wilson Steer, who was perhaps the last of the great water-colourists, surely deserves a paragraph all to himself.

It would be quite true to say that Wilson Steer was a superlative technician as well as being a very considerable artist, for he was one of the first painters of any originality to use water-colours in a really watery way for several decades. 'It may be a poor compliment,' Sickert wrote to him from Venice in 1895, 'but for all practical purposes the more experience I have, the more I find that the only things that seem to me to have a direct bearing on the practical purpose of painting my pictures are the things that I have learnt from you. To see the thing all at once. To work open and loose, freely, with a full brush and full colour. And to understand that when, with that full colour, the drawing has been got, the picture is done. It sounds nothing put into words, but it is everything put into practice.'

There have been other artists since Wilson Steer who have produced some very fine water-colour paintings and have exhibited and sold them, but it may be that the ideal conditions for water-colour painting belong to the past. As Ruskin pointed out, 'With the name of Richard Wilson the history of landscape art, founded on a genuine, meditative love of nature, begins for England.' With the decline of the native school of water-colour painters, it may truthfully be said to have finished. Certainly, the opportunities for quiet, meditative contemplation of the pastoral scene are much scarcer today than they used to be. If you decide to collect water-colour paintings, you will be reminded most happily of the charms of the English countryside as it was at its unspoiled best. In that, rather than in any lasting effect they may have had on the history of art, lies their true and most potent appeal.

7

COLLECTING DRAWINGS

USUALLY, an artist draws to store or convey information, or to work out his ideas, rather than to give enjoyment or to impress. That does not mean that all drawings are purely objective, but it may explain why a collection of drawings will always appeal to people who prefer the matter-of-fact clarity of a precise statement to the delicate nuances of a poetic suggestion.

It was not until the sixteenth century that it became fashionable to buy and keep drawings, but artists and connoisseurs have vied with each other ever since in their attempts to form collections that would be useful and informative, on the one hand, or decorative and valuable on the other. Frequently, a well-known artist of the past would exchange one or more of his drawings for a similar contribution from one of his contemporaries (Dürer is known to have effected an exchange of this kind with Raphael) and some artists, such as Rembrandt and Rubens, had formed massive collections by the ends of their lives. When such collections were bequeathed to a single lucky recipient, they stood a good chance of retaining their identity, and that is how the comprehensive collections of drawings by Domenichino remained intact, to find its way eventually to the Royal Collection at Windsor.

Among the great collections of drawings to be seen on the Continent are those at the Louvre, in Paris, which includes the magnificent collection formed by Louis XIV; at the Uffizi, in Florence, which includes the drawings collected by the members of the Medici family; at the Albertina, in Vienna; at the Hermitage, in Leningrad; and at the Kupferstichkabinet in Berlin. In Britain, there are notable collections of drawings at the British Museum, the Victoria and Albert Museum and

Sir John Soane's Museum in London; at the Ashmolean Museum at Oxford; and in the Royal Library at Windsor. The Duke of Devonshire's collection at Chatsworth is one of the most impressive still remaining in private hands.

Under all normal circumstances a drawing will be executed on paper of some kind (drawings on cloth, wood, bone, ivory or some other materials may come into your possession, but these will be rare). Therefore, you will find a certain familiarity with kinds of paper—and, possibly, an outline knowledge of the history of paper-making—extremely useful in forming a collection of drawings.

Paper, in a form not dissimilar to that we know now, was first produced in China nearly two thousand years ago.

Except in Egypt, where thin membranes stripped from the papyrus reeds were used for writing, parchment made from the skins of sheep and goats, and the finer-grained vellum made from the skins of calves and kids, were used for all manuscripts until the paper-making techniques developed by the Chinese had been introduced into the other parts of the world.

All the paper used for drawings in Western Europe during the Renaissance was made from cotton or linen rags. The rags were washed thoroughly, shredded and then pulped down with water until a thick white fluid, of an even consistency filled the vat. This fluid would then be poured out on to a tightly stretched cloth so that the surplus water could drain away (in recent centuries a wire mesh has been used in many cases instead of cloth). Then the residue would be pressed and dried, forming a tough, pliable sheet—with, sometimes, the mesh marks remaining to form a distinctive texture on the underside of the paper. This would then be treated with size to render it less absorbent.

Early in the nineteenth century it became customary, for economic reasons, to substitute wood pulp for rags, except when the paper to be produced was intended to be especially smooth and durable—as, for example, Whatman and other grades made specially for water-colour painting. After 1860 esparto grass was also used in paper manufacture. If an expert examines under a microscope a tiny scrap taken from a piece of paper he will usually be able to tell, to within a few years, when it was made.

That does not stop picture forgers producing specially 'aged' paper, though. Hogarth was fond of representing Time blowing smoke over the surface of a picture. He would not have been surprised to see a counterfeiter rolling, tearing and creasing a piece of paper intended to carry, later, an Old Master drawing, nor would he have raised his eyebrows if the same piece of paper were afterwards 'foxed' or stained in a convenient bath of cold coffee or tea. Sophisticated forgers use permanganate of potash and other chemicals to produce convincing blemishes, while diluted acid is sometimes used to simulate the appearance of a watermark.

Most of the drawings that may find their way into a collection will have been carried out in ink of some kind, with a pencil of some kind, or with chalks, pastels or crayons. Other methods are used, but it seems convenient to deal first with the artist's regular standbys.

The earliest inks were almost certainly made from charred bones, ground to powder and mixed with some gum solution that would act as a binder. In the Middle Ages, sepia inks, made from fluids produced by the cuttle fish, were widely used, and these were supplemented by inks made from iron salts of various kinds. Aniline inks were introduced in the second half of the nineteenth century. An expert is sometimes able to ascertain whether a drawing is genuine or not by making a chemical or spectroscopic examination of the ink deposits.

Ink drawings can be made with a brush of some kind, or with a pen. Chinese artists are by long tradition particularly skilful users of the brush, which they handle in a way that seems peculiar to occidental eyes—usually, they hold the brush at the opposite end to that normally held by the Westerner, and exercise what looks remarkably like 'remote control'.

The style of a pen drawing will clearly be influenced by the type of pen that the artist has chosen, the range of his choice being limited, of course, to the types available at the time the drawing was made. Medieval scribes and illuminators usually used pens cut from the quills of large birds such as swans and geese. Reeds, too, were trimmed to make sensitive drawing instruments. Metal pens do not appear to have been produced until late in the eighteenth century. Nowadays, artists use fountain pens, ball-point pens, and pens that feed ink on to paper through felt pads, according to their personal inclinations.

Pencils, in various grades from 8B (extremely soft) to 6H (extremely hard) are to be found in most artists' pockets nowadays, but these clean, portable and convenient accessories were not available in that exact form to Dürer, Da Vinci or Michelangelo. Until early in the reign of Queen Elizabeth I, chalks were most often used for rough sketches, and such pencils as there were had to be compounded from lead and tin. Graphite (sometimes called 'plumbago' or 'black lead') was then discovered at Borrowdale in the English Lake District, and its uses for drawing purposes were explored. The processes by which graphite could be ground down into a fine powder and recombined with refined clays to make 'leads' of various grades were not developed until 1760, when the family business of Faber was established at Nuremberg. In 1795 N. J. Conte devised a process whereby reconstituted graphite leads could be pressed into sticks and then fired in a kiln. Commercial pencil-making techniques are still based firmly on this method today.

Pastel drawings are usually conspicuous for the purity of their colouring. The sticks of colour are normally compressed without the addition of gum, oil or any other binding medium, so the pigments have no adulterant to reduce their intensity or to lower their tone. This method of manufacture has, however, two disadvantages—it makes the mixture of colours difficult, so that a large number of sticks have to be carried if the artist wishes to produce a wide range of hues, shades and tints. It makes the surface of pastel drawings peculiarly susceptible to damage, too, so if you add to your collection any drawings that you think may have been executed in this medium you will be well advised to see that they are properly glazed (to prevent smudging) and then hung in a place that is as free as possible from vibration. In an emergency a new lease of life can sometimes be given to a pastel drawing if a thin film of fixative (that is, white shellac dissolved in methylated spirit) is blown over it with a spray diffuser, but this is practically certain to impair the colours and should be avoided whenever possible.

Occasionally you may be offered for your collection a drawing that seems to have been executed with a particularly fine pencil, and contains lines of a specially beautiful quality. This may be a 'gold point' or a 'silver point' drawing, made with a piece of gold or silver wire on paper that has been given a wash of Chinese white. It is not a flexible technique— no line can be erased once it has been drawn—and nowadays it is seldom used.

That, then, is a brief list of the materials most commonly used for drawing, but, as may be expected, artists do not always arrange to work within such tidy limits. A good proportion of the drawings you will be offered for your collection will be carried out in a combination of two or more quite different materials. A pencil drawing may be given extra vitality by the addition of sepia shadows, for instance; an ink drawing may be reinforced with a water-colour wash; or a charcoal drawing on toned paper may have the high lights picked out with white chalk. The variety of methods used by different artists at different times and for different purposes can make even a small collection of drawings a source of almost inexhaustible interest. This may be an appropriate juncture to consider in more detail some of the different reasons that artists have for making drawings. The problems that he has to solve when he sits down to draw will determine the artist's approach.

First, there are 'pure' drawings—that is, drawings made for the purpose of recording observations, or for scientific study.

Throughout the Renaissance, Florence was the great centre of objective draughtsmanship, and detailed figure studies and portraits were produced in great numbers by artists as well known today as Domenico Ghirlandaio (1449–1494) and Sandro Botticelli (1444–1510). Once firmly established, the great European tradition of linear draughtsmanship took root in other countries besides Italy—eighteenth-century France produced Antoine Watteau, for instance, who was one of the most sensitive draughtsmen of all. Even as late as the nine-teenth century, 'pure' drawings were being executed with great skill by earnest students such as John Ruskin (1819–1900) and John Everett Millais (1829–1896), but study for study's sake seems to have become steadily less and less popular as the twentieth century has worn on. Today, an artist who could make a pictorial record of a subtle form with the economy and sensitivity of an Ingres or a Degas would be remarkable indeed.

'Working' drawings have been made by artists of all periods. When a painter is embarking on a large canvas or panel, it is obviously most expedient for him to carry out a small-scale design first. In the process of evolving this design, he may have to make several ancillary studies—each of the main figures in the composition may call for a drawing 'from life', for instance; the architectural setting, if there is one, may need checking; natural forms may be the better for careful analysis.

When incorporating his ancillary studies in the main cartoon, or when he finds it necessary to enlarge a drawing, the artist may use a system of 'squaring up'—that is, he may draw a network of faint lines over each of the surfaces with which he is concerned so that the lines divide those surfaces into a convenient number of squares or rectangles. By increas-ing or decreasing the size of the squares or rectangles in one of the networks he can enlarge or reduce, in an exactly deter-mined proportion, the drawing it is to contain.

Third on our list are drawings that have been used as a means of imaginative expression. Leonardo da Vinci was one of the earliest artists to exploit an extraordinary facility in what would be called nowadays a 'psychological' way.

Among many other draughtsmen with a subjective or romantic approach whose works are especially worth study is Henry Fuseli (1741–1825). Fuseli was born and brought up in Switzerland, and he did not settle permanently in England until he was thirty-eight years old. Fuseli might be aptly called 'the painter of nightmares', for most of his pictures, and the sketches he made for them, were imbued with the strange and the terrible. Madhouses, labyrinths and the nether regions formed appropriately theatrical settings for his haunting visions of monsters and the macabre. This is how Benjamin Robert Haydon (1786–1846) described a visit he made to Fuseli's workplace:

> 'I followed the maid into a gallery or showroom enough to frighten anybody at twilight. Galvanized devils—malicious witches brewing their incantations—Satan bridging Chaos, and springing upwards like a pyramid of fire—Lady Macbeth—Paolo and Francesca—Falstaff and Mrs Quickly —humour, pathos, terror, blood and murder, met one at every look! I expected the floor to give way—I fancied Fuseli himself to be a giant. I heard his footsteps and saw a little bony hand slide round the edge of the door, followed by a little white-headed, lion-faced man in an old flannel dressing-gown tied round his waist with a piece of rope and upon his head the bottom of Mrs Fuseli's work-basket . . .'

Fortunately for Fuseli, his pictures proved to be exactly in tune with the fashionable taste for the fantastic, the Gothic, and the picturesque, and he became a very popular figure. Even Blake, who was not always so tolerant of the successful and prosperous, wrote in his pocket book:

> *'The only Man that e'er I knew*
> *Who did not make me almost spue*
> *Was Fuseli: he was both Turk and Jew—*
> *And so, dear Christian Friends, how do you do?'*

The introduction of the steel pen nib at the end of the eighteenth century, with the subsequent development of different types of nib by the fiercely competitive manufacturers, led to an increased interest in pen and ink drawing. It led, too, to a widening variety in the types of line that artists could produce, but this, as Hesketh Hubbard has pointed out, 'was not entirely beneficial, for though it made possible greater delicacy and detail it also encouraged a spidery wiry line that lacked decorative value.' Of all the romantic draughtsmen who worked with pen and ink during Queen Victoria's reign,

15. On Dieppe Beach: a drawing by Aubrey Beardsley

Dante Gabriel Rossetti (1828–1882) was perhaps the most consistently successful. In his student days, Rossetti associated himself with Millais, Holman Hunt and a handful of other young artists in the formation of the Pre-Raphaelite Brotherhood, but his interest in medievalism and the exotic proved too strong for the tenuous bonds of sympathy that had brought the members of the Brotherhood together. 'D. G. Rossetti, you must understand,' wrote Millais after the two had drifted apart, 'was a queer fellow and impossible as a boon companion—so dogmatic and so irritable when opposed . . . At last, when he presented for our admiration the young women which have since become the type of Rossettianism, the public opened their eyes in amazement. "And this," they said, "is Pre-Raphaelitism!" It was nothing of the sort. The Pre-Raphaelites had but one idea—to present on canvas what they saw in Nature; and such productions as these were absolutely foreign to the spirit of their work.'

If Millais thought that Rossetti was a queer fellow, the mind positively boggles at what he must have made of Aubrey Beardsley (1872–1894) who was by any standards one of the oddest and most idiosyncratic artists ever thrown up by the end of a century. In his short life, which was terminated by tuberculosis, Beardsley produced a large number of highly original and, to some minds, slightly perverse drawings that were intended expressly for reproduction by the line block method, and for use as illustrations in 'quality' books. Whatever his merits as a draughtsman—and many people find the exaggerated posturings of his distorted figures difficult to bear—there can be no doubt at all about Beardsley's abilities as a designer. Each of his illustrations sits superbly on the page for which he intended it, and his wonderful sense of balance may do a lot to console us for the overcharged luxuriance of Beardsley's work and its general air of decadence.

After the morbid elegance of Beardsley's closed world, it may be a relief to turn to some artists in the fourth category in our list—those who have made drawings for purposes of social comment, satire or caricature. Of all works of art, drawings in this class are probably the greatest fun to collect.

In some companies one has only to mention the names Gillray, Rowlandson, Cruikshank and Ardizzone to raise an appreciative smile. All these men are, of course, to a greater or lesser extent spiritual descendants of Hogarth.

Thomas Rowlandson (1756–1827) was one of the most prolific artists there has ever been, in any medium—and one of the least inhibited. He was the son of a wealthy London tradesman, who encouraged the boy's early attempts to draw and paint and sent him to study at the Academy Schools. Unfortunately for Rowlandson, while he was thus occupied the father gambled away the family fortune, and the young artist found himself, on the threshold of manhood, compelled to support himself, entirely by his own talents, in the luxurious manner of life to which he had been accustomed.

Rowlandson seems to have been undeterred. Squandering blithely a fortune left him by a convenient French aunt, the young man started to produce with dazzling virtuosity the great series of robust and hilarious drawings with which we associate his name. Working, almost invariably, with a reed pen and wash or water-colour tint, he took his subjects gratuitously from scenes of contemporary life. Duchesses kissing butchers, bankers fondling barmaids, heiresses eloping with young Guards officers, sailors pursuing women and women pursuing sailors, noble ladies taking the waters at Bath, less noble ladies taking the waters in a tin tub—these and hundreds of other comic and near-comic figures are crowded exuberantly into Rowlandson's work until some of his drawings seem to be about to burst from their frames. Only one element in Rowlandson's artistic make-up may seriously disturb us—he had a tendency, seriously deplored by his publishers, to represent human beings as if they are some grosser kind of beast. Only rarely was this temptation allowed to get the better of him. On all normal occasions his pictures are jovial and witty and entirely without malice.

'Without malice' is certainly not a phrase that can be applied to the caustic drawings of James Gillray (1757–1815) and the popular engravings that were made from them. No one, not even the most blameless member of the Royal Family, was safe for long from the cruel cuts of Gillray's

16. 'The cat did it.' An etching by George Cruikshank which is
an amusing example of his work

lash, and many people who considered themselves vulnerable must have felt secretly relieved when the famous satirist's mind became demonstrably unhinged, and he had to be confined, for his own safety as well as that of the general public, in an upstairs room at his publisher's house.

A more balanced view of life, if one no less dramatic, was that taken by the brothers Robert and George Cruikshank (born 1789 and 1792 respectively). George Cruikshank is best known for his illustrations to Charles Dickens's *Sketches by Boz* and *Oliver Twist*, but these represent only a tiny fraction of his enormous output. Much of Cruikshank's early published work was etched. His pictures are notable for their extraordinary mingling of knockabout humour, grotesque ugliness and tender observation, and they are almost certainly, at the time of going to press, seriously under-valued.

There is no room here for a comprehensive list of late nineteenth- and twentieth-century book illustrators whose works may interest the picture collector, but it would not be reasonable to leave the subject without reminding the reader of the drawings of 'Phiz' (Hablot K. Browne, 1815–1882) who succeeded Cruikshank as the illustrator of Dickens's novels; Richard Doyle (1824–1883), perpetrator of the execrable series 'The Manners and Customs of ye Englyshe drawn from ye Quick' and other observations on the mid-Victorian scene; John Tenniel (1820–1914), best known for his illustrations for *Alice's Adventures in Wonderland* and *Through the Looking-Glass*, without which, to many people, these books would seem incomplete; Charles Keene (1823–1891) who was one of the most remarkable artists ever employed by *Punch*; George du Maurier (1834–1896) the recorder of the doings of High Society in Mayfair and elsewhere; George Belcher (1875–1947) the recorder of the doings of low society, mostly along the Bethnal Green Road; and, among contemporary artists who have preferred to work in a traditional style, Edward Ardizzone (born 1906). Ardizzone's talents have been employed by a number of publishers, and his free, spontaneous studies of children, animals, nursemaids and other picturesque oddities are among the most delightful acquisitions that can possibly be hung on a wall.

8

COLLECTING RELIEF AND INTAGLIO PRINTS

AN ORIGINAL work of art of any notable quality will always tend, under normal conditions of trade, to be expensive because it is the only one of its kind in existence. Etchings and engravings and other prints, on the other hand, are likely to fall within the scope of a much larger number of collectors, since their prices are only inflated in exceptional cases by some 'autograph' quality or quality of impression, or by rarity. By making a collection of prints you can get excellent examples of the works of many first-rate artists into your home, with a surprisingly small outlay.

Before you start buying prints in any quantity, though, you may find it helpful to know a little about the several different ways in which an impression can be made. Some printing techniques have a long history, others have been developed comparatively recently. All the techniques with which you as a collector will be primarily concerned fall under four main headings:

Relief printing. In relief printing, a block of some suitable material such as wood or metal is cut into or eroded so that some parts only of the flat, original surface are left raised. These parts are then coated with ink, the cut-away parts remaining clean. The print is made by transferring the image from the inked surfaces on to paper or some other receptive material—usually under considerable pressure.

Intaglio printing. In intaglio printing, cavities or recesses are made (by etching, engraving or some comparable process) in the flat surface of some suitable plate. These valleys or furrows are then filled with ink, the rest of the plate being wiped clean. The print is made by transferring the ink that has been trapped in the incisions on to damped paper or some

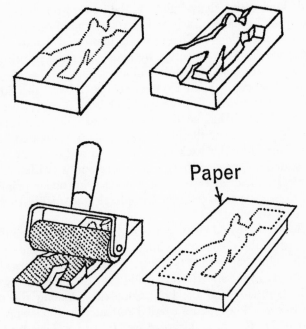

17. Relief printing

other receptive material—again, under considerable pressure.

Surface or *planographic printing*. This comparatively modern process, with *screen printing*, in which the ink is forced through a fine mesh of silk or synthetic material, will be described in Chapter 9.

WOODCUT PRINTING

This is probably the earliest form of relief printing, having been used by the Chinese at least as early as the ninth century A.D., so it should, clearly, be the first to be considered in detail.

In a woodcut, the design to be represented is drawn in reverse on the smooth, flat surface of a block of wood— usually a comparatively soft wood, such as apple or pear, cut along (as opposed to 'across') the grain. Then the outlines are defined with a sharp knife and the waste wood is removed with special gouges. Early woodcuts normally consisted of a series of black lines enclosing white unprinted shapes. These shapes would often be tinted by hand, after the printing ink was dry, with bold washes of colour.

When taking a print from a woodcut block, the normal practice is to work ink over the block with a roller so that a thin even film is left on the uncut surfaces. Then a piece of paper is placed over the block and pressure is applied—with a burnisher like the back of a spoon, in rudimentary workshops, or in a press of some kind where one is available. The technical difficulties of making a good print under primitive conditions give a charmingly unsophisticated quality to many medieval woodcuts.

The art of wood-cutting reached high levels during the first half of the sixteenth century, when artists of the calibre of Albrecht Dürer (1471–1528), Hans or John Burgkmair (*c*. 1473–*c*. 1531) and Hans Holbein (1497–1543) were working in Germany and the Low Countries. Among the most famous sets of woodcuts carried out at this time were the *Dance of Death* series, designed by Holbein and cut by Hans Lützelburger, and the great *Triumphal Arch and Car* and *Triumphal Procession*, undertakings commissioned by the Emperor Maximilian to immortalize his achievements. The Arch and Car were designed chiefly, if not wholly, by Dürer, the arch being cut on ninety-two blocks of wood, which, when placed together, measured more than 10 ft. by 9 ft. Unfortunately, early German woodcuts only rarely come on to the market, and when they do they command high prices.

Occasionally you may come across a colour woodcut that has been printed from more than one block, each hue, shade or tint requiring a separate impression or being produced by the superimposition of one colour on another. More rarely, you may see woodcuts in which the various colours have not been printed separately, but, instead, have been applied to different parts of the same block by hand, with brushes or 'dolly' pads. The Japanese are particularly clever at using this laborious technique.

18. A rhinoceros: from a woodcut by Albrecht Dürer, 1515

WOOD ENGRAVING

Wood engravings are not unlike woodcuts, but the slight differences in materials, tools and techniques used tend to allow finer drawing and more significant detail. Normally, the block is made from boxwood, which is very fine in texture and when cut takes a very clean edge. The surface used is invariably the one that has resulted from a cut made straight across the tree, and provides an excellent end-grain. Unfortunately the box tree grows very slowly and may take as much as three centuries to provide a trunk a foot across. Wood engravings tend, therefore, to be rather small.

19. A tool used for wood engraving

Wood engravings are not carried out with the knife and gouge technique used for woodcuts, but with specially designed tools that have the most engaging names—a 'graver' being used for cutting straight lines (Fig. 19), a 'spit-sticker' for curved lines and a 'scorper' or 'scauper' for clearing away unwanted wood. With sharp tools used with an easy movement of the hand a skilled engraver can produce a wide variety of beautiful surface textures.

There are several artists whose names are inevitably associated with wood engraving, among the best known being William Blake (1757–1827), who used this medium for a set of illustrations for *Virgil*; Edward Calvert (1799–1883), the romantic visionary; and during the twentieth century Robert Gibbings, Eric Ravilious and Joan Hassall.

But the wood engraver whose work is most generally known and loved was Thomas Bewick of Newcastle (1753–1827). His charming studies of natural life are masterpieces on a miniature scale and pack more genuine observation of the English countryside into a square inch than most artists spread over yards of canvas.

Bewick was not only a consummate draughtsman and a highly satisfactory designer, but he was also a great technical innovator. Before his time it was customary for the wood engraver (or the artist designing for a wood engraver) to draw with black lines on the wood block so that the white 'negative' shapes between these lines could be cut away. Bewick in many of his blocks reversed this process and instead cut the *lines* of his subject into the wood, producing in the print white lines upon a black background. The prints made from Bewick's blocks in which he combined both processes, contrasting each with the other, are of an unsurpassed richness and complexity.

Even if you are unable to afford prints taken directly from blocks designed by Dürer, Holbein and Bewick, you will find plenty of scope for collecting wood engravings in the innumerable examples carried out for books and magazines during the nineteenth century, before the development of photographic methods of reproduction made hand cutting redundant, except for the luxury undertakings of private presses. Many of these illustrations, notably those by the brothers Edward and Thomas Dalziel, John Swain, and W. J. Linton can still be picked up for a few pence from unsorted collections in unfashionable bric-à-brac shops, while others can be found in second-hand bookstalls, in the volumes in which they were originally published.

LINO CUTTING

This is the technique with which most schoolchildren learn the elementary principles of relief printing. Being almost as soft as soap, linoleum can be cut away with relatively harmless gouges and V-tools, but its cheesy consistency makes it quite unsuitable for any very fine work. However, in the hands of a bold designer it can be used for some strikingly decorative prints, and it is favoured by a few prominent poster artists.

LINE ENGRAVING

This is the most ancient of the intaglio processes and will be described first because the other techniques—etching, dry-point, aquatint, mezzotint and so on—are simply variants of this basic method.

Line engraving is normally carried out with a small tool called a 'graver' or 'burin'. This tool consists of a length of tempered steel, sharpened at one end to a fine point and fitted at the other end with a wooden handle. By this, pressure can be applied with the palm of the hand.

Several different kinds of metal have been used at various times for making the flat plates that are worked with the engraver's burin, but copper was the metal most consistently used until about 1820, when steel gradually superseded it— the harder metal being intended to yield a greater number of impressions from any plate. This is how a line engraving is made:

First, a number of furrows are ploughed in the flat, polished surface of the plate with the burin (many thousands of these lines may be needed to produce a small picture).

Then the plate is charged with ink—usually by some form of dabbing or smearing. After that, the polished surface is wiped clean so that ink remains only in the engraved lines. Then a sheet of paper is placed over the plate (usually it is a sheet that has been damped slightly to make it more work-able), a thick piece of cloth is placed over that, and then strong pressure is applied. A roller press is almost essential if the ink is to be transferred successfully on to the paper from the engraved lines in the plate.

Anyone who studies a good engraving closely will notice at once that much of its attractive quality is due to the varia-tion in the thickness of the lines—some parts being strong and dark; others, so thin and faint that they are barely perceptible. The engraver obtains this variation in one of two ways—by changing his burin (a tool that has been made out of a strip of metal with a square section will make a wider channel than a tool with a lozenge-section shank), or by changing the angle at which he holds it. A burin moving at a steep angle to the plate will tend to dig deeply and thus make a heavier line.

There are several other technical refinements that you may care to study if you are going to make a collection of engravings. For example, if you use a powerful magnifying glass you may be able to observe occasionally the effects of the 'burr' or ragged serration pushed up by the burin on either side of the line it is engraving (normally this burr would be removed by the engraver with a special scraping tool). Under this really close scrutiny, too, you can hardly fail to admire the wonderful craftsmanship of the commercial engravers of the eighteenth and nineteenth centuries, who hatched, splattered and stippled their plates with incredible virtuosity.

The finest and rarest engravings, such as the portraits of William Faithorne and his seventeenth-century contemporaries, which are of great historical interest, tend to be rather expensive, but there are many other respected engravers whose work you can look out for and collect without having to make too great an outlay. It is still possible to pick up for a few shillings prints in good condition from the superb series issued by William Hogarth (1697–1764). 'Subjects,' Hogarth observed, 'I considered as writers do. My picture was my stage, and men and women my actors who were by means of certain actions and expressions to exhibit a dumb show.' His paintings and engravings are full of amusing detail and give a wonderful picture of what life may have been like in eighteenth-century London. Here is a key to some of Hogarth's most admired prints:

The Harlot's Progress. This is the first series of 'morality' pictures that brought Hogarth fame and fortune after a frustrating chain of delays and disappointments (an advertisement in the *Country Journal* in January 1732 announced that 'The AUTHOR of the Six COPPER PLATES, representing a

Harlot's Progress, being disappointed of the Assistance he proposed, is obliged to engrave them all himself, which will retard the Delivery of the Prints to the Subscribers about two months . . .').

1. Moll arrives in London by slow coach from the country and is immediately picked up by an evil woman. (Hogarth's contemporaries recognized this crone as being an exact portrait of Mother Needham, a notorious bawdy-house keeper who had been recently sentenced to stand in the pillory.)

2. Moll, now a kept woman, gives way to tantrums, which alarm her protector.

3. Moll at a belated breakfast. In the shadows in the background of this print we can see the figure of Sir John Gonson, the relentless Westminster magistrate, who has evidently arrived at Moll's sordid quarters on a 'raid'. (The Lords of the Treasury were so eager to obtain copies of this print, with its portrait of their colleague, that they suspended their meeting and trooped off to Hogarth's.)

4. Moll in Bridewell, the House of Correction, where harlots were sent to serve terms of hard labour.

5. Moll, some years later, in an advanced stage of a loathsome disease, the consequences of her profession.

6. Moll's funeral. The only mourners are her little son, who is more interested in his new spinning top, and a few rather dilapidated ladies of the town.

The Rake's Progress. Hogarth intended this series, published in 1735, to extend his income considerably, as well as his reputation, since the Copyright Act, passed earlier in that year almost entirely by Hogarth's efforts, would give adequate protection against 'pirates'.

1. Tom Rakewell, having inherited a fortune, takes formal possession of the home of his dead ancestor, whose personal papers and chattels are still littered around the apartment.

2. Tom holds a levée. A tailor, a dancing master, a prize fighter and two musicians pander to the young heir's growing self-importance.

3. Supper at the Rose Tavern. Tom turns to the fair sex for relaxation and pleasure.

4. Tom, alighting from a sedan chair, is arrested for debt. (Anyone familiar with St. James's Street today will immediately recognize the setting Hogarth used for this incident.)

5. To improve his fortunes, Tom makes a mercenary marriage with a woman who is wealthy, elderly and unprepossessing.

6. Tom gambles his wife's fortune away.

7. Tom in a debtors' prison. He is tormented by the reproaches of his one-eyed wife.

8. Tom in Bedlam, the public madhouse for paupers. This is a haunting picture of human decay.

The Marriage-à-la-Mode: Announced in the London *Daily Post* in April 1743, in these terms: 'MR HOGARTH intends to publish by Subscription, SIX PRINTS from Copper-Plates, engrav'd by the best Masters in Paris, after his own Paintings; representing a Variety of *Modern Occurrences* in *High-Life* . . .'

1. A contract is drawn up by lawyers, arranging a marriage between the daughter of a rich merchant and the young heir to an ancient but impoverished earldom.

2. The pair at breakfast. Disillusion and boredom are already wrecking the marriage.

3. The young husband visits, with a paramour who is little more than a child, the establishment of a notorious quack pox-doctor.

4. The Countess holds court in her richly decorated dressing-room. She is surrounded by male spongers and parasites.

5. The Earl surprises his wife in bed with another man. He is killed in the ensuing quarrel.

6. Suicide of the Countess. Her father, careful as well as wealthy, removes the wedding ring from the finger of the dead girl. (Through a leaded casement window we get an excellent view of Old London Bridge, which was still standing, overburdened with ancient and dilapidated buildings, when Hogarth made his sketches for this scene.)

There are many other splendid prints published from Hogarth's workshop that collectors look out for. These include *A Midnight Modern Conversation* and *The Laughing Audience* (1733); *Southwark Fair* (1735); *A Consultation of*

Physicians, *The Sleeping Congregation* and *The Distressed Poet*
(1736); *Four Times of the Day* and *Strolling Actresses dressing
in a Barn* (1738); *Industry and Idleness* (1747); *Calais Gate*,
or '*O the Roast Beef of Old England*' (1749); and *Beer Street*,
Gin Lane and *The Four Stages of Cruelty*, all issued in 1751.

ETCHING

This is a process that is almost as old as line engraving, for
it was experimented with by several artists during the sixteenth century and was widely and most impressively used in
the seventeenth century, when its resources were stretched
to their uttermost limits by one of the greatest artists of all
time, Rembrandt van Rijn. It is a process that has been more
popular with creative artists, since its general development,
than line engraving, for it does not demand quite so much
mechanical dexterity and leaves the mind freer to deal with
problems of design and representation.

Etching, like line engraving, is an intaglio process, and is
usually carried out on a copper plate. The plate is first cleaned
and polished, and then it is covered with a thin film of wax
and bitumen. The etcher 'fixes' this by holding the plate over
a low flame so that the warmth can melt the wax, and then
he blackens the ground by holding the plate over a succession
of lighted tapers. This is done so that he can see exactly what
is happening when he starts work with a needle.

That, then, is the next stage, and in it all the etcher's
powers of design and draughtsmanship are called into play.
He may work from preliminary sketches or he may draw
directly on to the plate, but whichever method he uses, his
aim will be to cut through the protective coating with the
point of his needle and to expose the surface of the metal.
Whether his work is sketchy or exact, or tentative or bold,
he will find his etching needle an extremely sensitive drawing
instrument.

Next come the operations by which the exposed parts of
the metal are eaten away, to make the same kind of ink-
retaining channels in the surface of the plate as would be
made by a line engraver's burin.

A Japanese print by Hokusai: *Sekiya Village on the Sumida River*

Another print by Hokusai: *Temma Bridge in Osaka*

First, the back and sides of the plate are given a protecti
coat of varnish. Then it is placed in a dish of acid (usually, a
dilute solution of nitric acid is used) and the process of erosion
begins. The length of the immersion depends, of course, on
the strength of the acid, but it is normally only a matter of
minutes. This is usually known as the 'first etch'.

Then, the plate may be washed to stop the action of the
acid, and all the lines that are to be fine or faint in the finished
print are covered or 'stopped out' with varnish. The plate is
then returned to the acid bath, and all the lines that are still
unprotected are given another brief period of erosion.

Clearly, this process can be repeated several times, the
lines being etched more deeply, so that they will be more and
more distinct in the finished print, each time the plate is
returned to the bath. You will realize the uses of this if you
examine closely any of the 'Thames Set' etchings of James
McNeill Whistler (1834–1903). In the prints made from his
plates the effects of distance are represented superbly by the
artist's control of the strength of each line.

When the darkest lines (usually those that are to be in the
foreground of the picture) have been etched sufficiently
deeply, the plate is washed again, and the protective ground
and varnish are removed with methylated spirit and turpentine. Then a print or 'proof' is made in the same way as a
print is made from a line engraving. This is usually referred
to as a 'first state' print.

Etching, as a process, is most conveniently flexible. If the
artist decides, on looking at the first state proof, that he
wishes to alter or correct any part of his design, or to do any
additional drawing, he can lay a fresh ground and do further
work into it. By this means he can produce 'second state'
prints, and 'third state' prints, and so on, to perfection. Print
collectors find it instructive to compare the prints taken from
a plate in its various states, and thus to follow the progressive
stages by which a great etcher like Rembrandt carried his
work forward until he was as near to being satisfied with it
as he would ever be.

If you buy a print taken from an etched plate, you will probably find that it is both signed by the artist and numbered.

20. A young woman reading: an etching by Rembrandt van Rijn

Normally, the figures in the margin indicate the number of prints produced in that edition, separated by a stroke from the number of that impression in order of printing.

SOFT GROUND ETCHING

This is a special form of etching used by Gainsborough, Turner and several modern artists to produce prints that are

generally softer and hazier than those made from plates
etched in the ordinary way with a needle.

As the name suggests, the artist first applies a soft ground
to the warmed plate, using tallow or vaseline with the wax
and bitumen to prevent it hardening. Then he puts a thin
piece of paper over this ground and carries out a drawing on
it with a pencil, exactly as if he is carrying out a straightforward studio sketch. When he pulls the paper away, parts
of the ground will adhere to the back of it, leaving the surface
of the plate exposed wherever he has applied pressure with
the pencil.

The plate is etched, and the prints are made from it, as
described for an ordinary line etching.

DRYPOINT

This is a technique that produces very distinctive prints. No
ground is applied to the plate, but the drawing or design is
ploughed directly into the surface with a specially hard point
—a steel, diamond or sapphire point is most often used.

The characteristically soft, dark, rich quality of a drypoint
print is due to the small burrs of waste metal pushed up by
the hard point as it is driven across the surface of the plate.
These burrs are not removed by the artist, but they are left,
and help to retain additional ink when a print is made. Unfortunately, they tend to wear away rather quickly, so it is
most unusual for a drypoint plate to retain its best print-
making qualities for more than a few impressions unless it is
subjected to a special hardening process.

The drypoint technique is frequently used by artists for
strengthening and giving extra pictorial value to certain
small but important areas of plates etched in the orthodox
way.

AQUATINT

An aquatint is an etching which may include tones (that is,
degrees of lightness and darkness) as well as lines. It is not
an easy technique to employ, which may explain why it has
had relatively few practitioners.

Usually, the delightful 'granulated' effects of an aquatint are produced by the deposition of minute particles of resin or asphaltum, which are blown or shaken over the surface of the plate and allowed to settle. The plate is then warmed so that the particles melt and adhere to it. Clearly, the acid will etch the metal away only where it is not protected by the minute resin or asphaltum droplets.

The difference between the varying degrees of lightness and darkness in each of the areas of the plate is controlled by a complicated series of 'stopping out' operations.

MEZZOTINT

This is an engraving technique in which varying tones are produced by the use of a rocking tool fitted with dozens of tiny hard teeth. As this tool is worked slowly and in different directions over the surface of the plate, it produces a texture not unlike that of a sponge—except of course, that the holes are much smaller. If inked up in that state, the whole plate would produce a very dark tone. To complete his design, the artist works slowly over the surface of the plate with a scraping tool, depressing the raised burrs where he wishes the tone to be a little lighter, and burnishing the surface where he wants a 'high light'—that is, where little ink is to be left on the paper at all.

The general principles of mezzotint engraving were discovered about 1642 by one Ludwig von Siegen, who was a soldier in the service of William VI, Landgrave of Hesse-Cassel, and were further developed by Prince Rupert (of Civil War fame) after von Siegen had demonstrated his method to that eminent cavalry officer. After the Restoration of the Monarchy, the technique was introduced into Britain and proved so popular with artists and their patrons that it was promptly dubbed by the French *la manière anglaise*.

Mezzotint engraving was used throughout the late seventeenth, eighteenth and nineteenth centuries for reproducing important oil-paintings, and some of the early portraits of notabilities are of considerable value to historians. The great masters of the Georgian era—Reynolds, Romney and Gainsborough—were particularly well served by the mezzotinters, for the works of those painters seemed particularly well suited to bring out the best qualities of the secondary technique, and the artists and engravers worked in close collaboration. Few mezzotints can be truly described as original works of art, but the best of them have a delicacy and charm of their own which makes them well worth collecting.

BAXTER PRINTS

These are pictures carried out by a special process invented and patented by George Baxter (1804–1867). They were at one time much sought after by connoisseurs and are still worth hunting for today, though some people find their sentimentality—many of them deal with martyrdoms and missionary-cookings and other unfashionable subjects—a little oppressive.

Baxter was the son of a printer who employed skilled craftsmen to colour by hand the pictures he was preparing for publication. The son, however, determined to find a more economical way of colouring prints, and by 1835 he had developed his new mechanical system. Baxter's method was somewhat laborious. First, he would print a tonal version of the picture, using an aquatint or mezzotint plate charged with brown, blue-grey, or some other neutral colour. Then he would print more positive colours over this, using one engraved wood block for each hue, shade or tint (sometimes he would use as many as twenty different blocks to print one picture). The oil-based inks he used produced some rich effects, so that a genuine Baxter print can be easily mistaken for an oil-painting if it is not looked at closely.

Baxter was invited to display his work at the Great Exhibition of 1851, and was awarded a prize. In the next year he published his masterpiece *Gems of the Great Exhibition*. In spite of its success, Baxter's business failed and the patents passed out of his hands.

PURCHASING PRINTS WISELY

Having become acquainted with the various techniques by

which prints can be produced, and having made a close study
of good examples of each—if possible with a strong magnifying glass—you may well decide to start a specialized collection: that is, one in which prints of one particular kind, or
of one period, or from one country, predominate. Whatever
the range of your collection, there are certain basic principles
that you may care to bear in mind when you are purchasing
prints, for the value of your collection, and the pleasure you
will get from it, will be directly governed by the care you
take in selecting the examples to include.

The first factor to be considered is the general condition
of the print. Obviously a torn, cropped or sheared print is not
going to be as valuable as one that is in a mint state, nor is a
print that has been blurred by rubbing, or 'backed' (that is,
stuck down on another piece of paper) or 'laid down' (that is,
stuck down on strawboard or cardboard). Ideally, every print
you purchase should look as nearly as possible as if it has just
come straight from the press.

Then, you should scrutinize closely two features that will
occur in all normal prints made from flat plates, such as
engravings and etchings.

The first is the 'margin' or band of plain paper that surrounds the impression. Many collectors are willing to pay
higher prices for old prints that have wide and unsoiled
margins, and this has led to a certain amount of counterfeiting
—with care, a print can be trimmed back right to the edge of
the printed surface, and this can then be carefully inlaid into
a recess cut in a new—and spurious—mount.

The second special feature to notice is the 'plate mark'—
the indentation in the paper made by the edge of the sheet of
metal from which the print has been taken. There are two
points to notice about this. The first is that a plate mark may
be a rough guide to the age of a print, since the edges of
modern copper and steel plates are nearly always finished off
with a bevel, while the edges of really old ones (say previous
to 1800) were always unbevelled. The second is purely negative—occasionally, you will come across a print that appears
to have no plate mark at all! Prints of this kind are not necessarily forgeries—they may have been commissioned for use

as book illustrations and engraved on plates larger than the pages on which they were to appear: so, when the margins of the book were trimmed, the plate marks were cut away.

Unfortunately for the amateur, the light-fingered gentlemen who try to turn a dishonest penny by faking and forging have never been slow to turn their attention to the conveniently profitable print-making processes.

There are various ways in which you can guard against wasting your money on spurious examples, if you decide to collect prints. Holding every print you are offered up to a strong light is one safeguard. Sometimes an unscrupulous person will have repaired a damaged print by inlaying a small patch of paper, and by re-drawing the missing lines with small strokes of a pen. While this can hardly be described as whole-scale forgery, it is a practice that can make a previously unsaleable print saleworthy—to the uninitiated.

Clearly, if the original block or plate has survived, fresh impressions can be taken from it should it fall into the hands of a dishonest person. In the case of etchings and engravings, these impressions will never be any clearer than the impressions taken during the artist's lifetime—unless, that is, an attempt is made to give fresh life to the plate by re-etching or re-engraving it, and as this is an operation that needs great skill the results of such interference are, to an expert's eye, usually immediately apparent. In most cases, any parts of a plate that have been re-engraved or re-etched will produce, in later prints, lines that are over-distinct and out of key with the rest of the picture.

Even if a block or plate has survived in first-rate condition, a dishonest person will not find it easy to pass off modern impressions as original prints unless he (or she) is able to obtain some contemporary paper. The paper used for genuine eighteenth-century prints now feels soft and silky when compared to modern papers, which are relatively hard and harsh. When you have had a little experience of handling prints you will soon sense if paper is 'wrong'.

Among the many attractive prints often to be found for sale at moderate prices in antique shops are those executed in the laborious 'stipple engraving' technique by Francesco

Bartolozzi (1727–1815) and his numerous pupils. In this method, small dots and needle pricks were used to build up the forms instead of the lines and hatchings found in ordinary engravings, and it proved to be eminently suitable for reproducing small portraits of aristocratic or amorous women, and similar subjects that required a certain sensuousness of approach. In 1802 Bartolozzi was persuaded to leave England to take charge of the National Academy at Lisbon and he lived in Portugal for the rest of his life. But 'Bartolozzi' plates and prints went on being produced in England in great quantities after the Master had left. Look closely at any Bartolozzi print you are offered and you may see that it bears the inscription 'Engraved by Bartolotti'. Any print that bears this legend cannot be genuine, though it may still be very attractive.

Fortunately for the amateur print-collector, there is at least one excellent standard work of reference that is readily available. A copy of Whitman's *Print-Collector's Handbook*, which was revised and enlarged by Malcolm Salaman and is published by George Bell & Sons, Ltd., of London, contains several hundred pages of valuable information about prints of all kinds.

9

COLLECTING LITHOGRAPHS AND
SCREEN PRINTS

A WIDE new field of activity was opened to picture-makers at the end of the eighteenth century when Alois Senefelder discovered that prints could be made from flat slabs of stone.

Senefelder is known to have been an actor and playwright as well as a dabbler in various elementary printing processes. One day—the story goes—he obtained some smooth flat pieces of Kellheim stone to act as surfaces on which he could grind his colours. While he was busy with one of these, his mother hurried into his workshop and asked him, as the washerwoman had called, to write down her laundry list. Senefelder had no paper and ink handy, so he wrote the list on the stone with some of his oily printing ink. When, later, he needed to clean the stone he got one of the rare, brilliantly inventive ideas which seem so obvious to those with the advantage of hindsight—he decided to see if he could etch away the background shapes of the stone with nitric acid, leaving the writing to remain at its original level so that he could take a print from it.

His initial experiments were not, in fact, successful, but in the course of them he discovered an alternative method of preparing the stone for printing that involved no etching away—he saw how he could use the natural antipathy of oil and water to produce areas that were attractive to ink and repellent to ink, respectively, on one absorbent surface. As this discovery forms the basis of all subsequently developed lithographic techniques it should be described in a little detail.

Let us suppose that an artist wishes to make by the traditional methods a lithographic print of—say—a landscape design of which he is particularly fond.

First, he will select a suitable stone. This will be a calcareous oolite, or limestone, and will have been formed on the bed of the sea during the Jurassic period some 150,000,000 years ago. All kinds of interesting fossils have been found in limestone deposits of this period, but the artist looks for a stone that is as far as possible flawless. It should be of equal thickness over the whole of its area, and it should be so thick that it will be in no danger of cracking when it is under strain in the press. You will appreciate that a wholly satisfactory lithographic stone tends to be heavy!

Having chosen his stone, the artist will next make sure that it is perfectly clean and level. He does this by rubbing a block of gritstone, or pumice, over the whole of the surface on which he is going to draw. If the stone has been used for printing before, he will have to use a second and slightly smaller stone with some powdered flint or coarse carborundum abrasive to remove all traces of the previous work. Sand and water are used as a grinding paste to produce the finished surface or 'grain'.

Next, he will wash the stone thoroughly and dry it. Then it will be ready for him to draw on. Usually he will use for this a specially made lithographic chalk which will contain soap, wax, tallow and other substances. Its most characteristic quality will be its greasiness.

As he draws on the stone with this chalk, the greasy substance will be driven into the pores in the upper surface. The grease may penetrate into the stone for some appreciable depth—to stop it spreading outwards, parallel to the surface of the stone, the artist will 'fix' it with a treatment of fresh gum arabic solution. This solution enters the pores of the stone and effectively seals it off from the intrusions of grease or any other oily substance. A lithographer refers to this sealing-off process as 'de-sensitization'. When the gum has dried, he will probably wash off with liberal douches of clean water those parts of it that remain on the upper surface of the stone.

When his drawing is complete and the unmarked stone is wholly de-sensitized, the artist will wash away the greasy crayon deposits from the surface of the stone with turpentine. To the uninitiated it may seem quite senseless to remove a drawing that has only just been made, but the purpose of this operation is rather subtle—the turpentine does NOT remove the grease that is concealed in the stone: it removes only the superficial markings.

Before any prints can be made, the artist has to make sure that the stone is still soaked with water, and he will re-moisten it, with a sponge or a damp cloth, if it shows any tendency to become dry.

Then he charges a roller with printing ink and rotates it over the surface of the stone. Where the roller comes into contact with any part of the stone that is still wet (that is, with water), no ink will be transferred from the roller to the stone. Wherever the roller comes into contact with any part of the surface that contains grease, ink will be transferred at once. In this way the artist produces on the surface of the stone an exact reproduction, in wet printing ink, of the draw-ing or design he carried out originally in lithographic chalk.

To transfer this drawing or design on to paper, the artist will need a special press. Usually this will be made of cast iron and will have a reinforced wooden bed on which the stone is placed. When a sheet of suitable paper has been placed over the inked surface of the stone, pressure is applied by means of a long, straight, leather-edged scraper that is pulled across a protective 'tympanum' over its upper surface. When the sheet of paper is removed from the stone there should be on it—if the press has been adjusted correctly—an exact reproduction, in reverse, of the original drawing made with lithographic chalk on the surface of the stone. By re-inking the stone, and repeating the printing process, the artist can obtain a second reproduction of the drawing, and so on.

Since Senefelder's time there have been only a few minor developments in the basic technique of lithography, the one most helpful to the artist-printer being, perhaps, the substi-tution of light zinc or aluminium plates for heavy blocks of stone.

Obviously, a metal plate is not absorbent like oolitic lime-stone, so when an artist draws with a greasy chalk on one he will expect to leave only a thin film of water-repellent material on the outside surface, and he may not be able to obtain prints quite as rich and 'contrasty' as those he can obtain from a stone. The greater convenience of working on light plates is, however, thought by most artists to compensate for this.

Clearly, prints can be taken from a plate or stone in any required colour, instead of black, as long as the necessary ink is available. It is possible to produce prints with two, three and more colours, too, as long as a separate stone or plate is used for each colour, and as long as the printing surfaces are correctly 'registered' for every impression. Where one colour is printed over another, a third colour is normally produced (yellow printed on blue may make green, to take a fairly straightforward example). Modern colour lithographs offer a very rewarding field for the picture collector of comparatively modest means, since they are nearer to being original works of art than mechanical reproductions, but they are usually sold at prices which are small fractions of the prices charged for oil-paintings or water-colours by the same artists.

The first really prominent artist to use lithography as a serious means of expression was the Spaniard Francisco Goya y Lucientes (1746–1828). Goya was a great painter and portraitist as well as being one of the most ruthless satirists who ever handled an etching needle. He was already well advanced in years and comparatively infirm when he made his first experiments with Senefelder's new process, but he found that the technique suited him, and he used it to produce some memorable prints when, in the last years of his life, he settled down in voluntary exile in Bordeaux.

French artists have always taken kindly to lithography, two of its earliest exponents being those two great leaders of the Romantic Movement—Jean Louis Géricault, who died in 1824 at the premature age of thirty-three, having lithographed in his fevered life some very impressive studies of horses, and Ferdinand Victor Eugène Delacroix (1798–1863) his friend, whose eminence and authority conferred a certain dignity on the new technique, and, at the same time, helped to popularize it. As interested in literature and drama as he was in the visual arts, Delacroix found the most potent stimulus for his creative activity in the poems of Dante and the plays of Shakespeare, in medieval history, and, later, in barbarous and exotic tales from the untamed Orient. The set of 'Faust' subjects that he issued in 1828 was one of the most ambitious projects undertaken in the early days of lithography.

Honoré Daumier (1808–1879) was another great French artist whose name is inevitably linked with lithography. It is inevitably associated with the city of Paris, too, for the Daumier family moved there when Honoré was a child, and the boy grew up as deeply imbued with the atmosphere of the city as was Charles Dickens with the atmosphere of London.

It did not take Daumier long to learn the technique of lithography, and once he had explored its resources he used it to produce an unsurpassable record of the vagaries of human behaviour. By 1830, he was managing to support himself by doing anonymous work for various publishers, but in that year his talent for producing satirical political cartoons attracted the notice of Charles Philipon, a liberal journalist who had founded, and was the proprietor of, *La Caricature*. Philipon invited Daumier to contribute some work to his paper and thus started one of the longest and most fruitful partnerships in the whole history of the visual arts.

It was a partnership that was interrupted temporarily, though, almost as soon as it had begun, when Daumier was rash enough to represent, in one of the lithographs he drew for Philipon, Louis Philippe in the guise of Gargantua. Outraged by this act of *lèse-majesté*, the authorities locked Daumier away for six months and forced Philipon to cease publication of *La Caricature*. However, Philipon had an ebullient personality, and unabashed he started a new publication which he called *La Charivari*, with the avowed intention of using it to ridicule the evils of society. Among these, of course, he included the authorities and Louis Philippe.

The lithographs Daumier produced for *La Charivari* in the 1840s and 1850s are among the most trenchant condemnations of human folly that have found pictorial expression in any medium. The more effete members of the legal profession made particularly rewarding targets for his wit, and the studies he made in the courts, in the interiors of railway carriages, and in the homes of the poor are really important social documents.

Unfortunately, Daumier's eyesight began to fail when he was in his early sixties, and by 1878 he was living in poverty, and totally blind. His friends, led by the painters Corot and Daubigny and the dealer Durand-Ruel, organized an exhibition of his works, but it met with little success. Since his death, in the following year, his works have gained in popular appeal and his lithographs are now eagerly sought.

Another French artist whose lithographs are extremely popular with collectors is Henri de Toulouse-Lautrec (1864–1901). Toulouse-Lautrec was a member of an ancient family who became interested in drawing and painting at a comparatively early age and was considered by his more sporting kinsmen to be a little eccentric for wasting his time on such effeminate pursuits. When he was fifteen, he suffered two serious accidents which left him permanently crippled and deformed, and there is no doubt that his serious physical disabilities affected his mode of living, his relationships with other people, and his art.

When he was twenty-two, Toulouse-Lautrec settled in Montmartre; having plenty of money to squander, he was able to spend a great deal of time in the dance halls of the Moulin de la Galette and Moulin Rouge, in the low bars and brothels with which the district was plentifully supplied, and at the circus. Through his work we can get to know the physical appearance of so many *fin-de-siècle* stars—the dancers La Goulue and Jane Avril, the singers Yvette Guilbert, May Belfort and May Milton—almost as well as if they are personal acquaintances of ours. (We can get to know a whole crowd of the local pimps, thugs and prostitutes, too, for Toulouse-Lautrec was, for an aristocrat, surprisingly unfussy about the company he kept.)

It has been estimated that Toulouse-Lautrec produced more than three hundred and fifty lithographs, besides much other work, in ten hectic years of artistic activity. His prints, many of which were created from memory while he was receiving treatment for acute alcoholism, were strikingly original. Set, as often as not, in the cabarets, music halls and circuses of which he was so fond, each would have some feature—usually a single figure or animal placed in a domi-nating position in the picture area—that fixes it ineradicably in the memory. His use of silhouetted shapes and his readi-ness to exploit a wide variety of surface textures that he could contrast with these had a profound influence on a group of young and progressive artists who are usually associated with him. Pierre Bonnard (1867–1947), Jean Edouard Vuillard (1868–1940) and Louis Anquetin (1861–1932) are perhaps the best known of these, but the collector with a taste for the bizarre qualities of that period may be especially attracted to the works of Théophile Alexandre Steinlen (1836–1900).

Meanwhile, in other parts of the world, lithography was becoming increasingly popular, both for artistic and com-mercial purposes, notably in America and England.

The new process was introduced into the New World and developed there, chiefly to satisfy the demand for informative or exciting illustrations that could be cheaply produced in comparatively large quantities. The landscape studies of Bass Otis and the hand-coloured prints in the smaller edition of Audubon's *Birds of America* are early examples that collectors are prepared to pay considerable sums to possess. A little later the celebrated firm of Currier and Ives commenced its activities. Under the inspiration of the two energetic partners Nathaniel Currier and James Merritt Ives, many series of prints were issued, depicting national calamities, political figures, sporting events and other popular subjects, and these sold in great numbers. Nowadays the history of the American nation and its development to its present status as a great world power make a theme with which transatlantic collectors are much in sympathy, and Currier and Ives prints are not, in consequence, undervalued.

In England, lithography was not widely favoured by artists until its resources had been demonstrated (and talked about) by that inimitable propagandist James McNeill Whistler. Whistler's best work combined in an extraordinarily success-ful way the visual truth sought for by the French Impres-sionists with the impeccable design of the best Japanese prints. He was working on his well-known series of Thames-side studies, or 'Nocturnes', when he was persuaded to turn his hand to lithography. The prints that resulted had an immediate appeal, and before many years had passed lithography was as popular a process with English artists as etching. The formation in 1910 of the Senefelder Club, which has included among its members artists as varied, and as distinguished, as Sir Frank Brangwyn, Augustus John, C. R. W. Nevinson, Charles Shannon and, from France, J. Forain, Fantin La Tour and Henri Matisse, has ensured that works of a high standard have been regularly brought to the attention of the public and sold. The club, at the time of going to press, is known as the 'Senefelder Group of Artist Lithographers'.

Lithography, then, is a comparatively new development in the field of the Fine Arts, but it will be seen, from what has been written so far in this chapter, that it is an extremely healthy one. The number of contemporary artists who publish original lithographs in reasonably large editions is so great that it would be impossible to quote the names of more than a tiny percentage of them in a book of this length. Perhaps the most famous artist of recent years to draw directly on to stones is Pablo Picasso. A print from that master's hand is worth a place in a collection for its autograph interest alone.

SCREEN PRINTS

Screen printing is now widely used for commercial purposes —fabric designs, posters, showcards, labels and many other repetitive features required in the home or by trade are produced with this technique. It is also used by many artists— being especially popular in the United States—and it is sometimes referred to as 'serigraphy'.

It would be less confusing, perhaps, to refer to 'these techniques' instead of using the word in the singular, for there are several different variations on the method, and each artist will choose the one that suits him—or her—best.

Normally, a piece of finely woven silk material is stretched tightly over a wooden frame. If a piece of paper is put down on a flat working surface, and this silk sheet is placed over it,

England is the home of landscape painting in water-colours—but some of the most striking pictures were by artists 'on tour'. *Snowdon;* an unfinished study by John Varley (1778–1842)

Jack in his Glory: a lively work from the eighteenth century by Julius
Caesar Ibbetson (1759–1817)

it will clearly be possible to press black or coloured ink through the silk on to the paper by exerting only a small amount of pressure—usually with a rubber tongue or 'squeegee'. The artist makes a design, then, by covering some parts of the silk screen or by rendering them so impermeable that they will not allow the ink to pass through. Then, the paper will receive the ink only where the artist has deliberately left the silk screen in its original sieve-like state.

The effectiveness of the different methods employed by silk screen printers depends on the material or materials used for 'stopping out'. In one of the more straightforward processes, pieces of paper or plastic can be placed under the silk before the ink is pressed through it, so that these will act in the same way as the negative shapes of a child's stencil.

In a variation of this method, a coat of gum and water is used, instead of paper or plastic, to act as the 'sealer'.

There is a more involved variation still, in which the drawing is made directly on to the silk with a greasy chalk. Then the screen is coated with gum. Finally, the whole surface is wiped over with turpentine. This removes the original chalk of the drawing, with any gum that may be adhering to it, but it leaves the rest of the fabric still coated with gum, and impermeable. Then, when ink is pressed over the screen, it will pass only through those parts of the silk that were once (before the turpentine wash) covered with chalk. The effects that can be obtained with this last method are not unlike those that result from lithographic processes.

10

COLLECTING SPORTING PICTURES

In any country that has been for many centuries predominantly agricultural, a general interest in field sports can almost be taken for granted. It is not surprising, then, that a large number of British artists who were working before the Industrial Revolution turned to hunting, shooting, fishing, horse racing, coursing and other outdoor pastimes almost automatically for their subject-matter. A collection of sporting paintings and prints can be both valuable and attractive, and it can be guaranteed to increase in interest as the land becomes steadily more and more urbanized, and as the sight of a partridge covey and the sound of a hunting horn become remote, far-off memories of the past.

As a rough guide, you can divide any original sporting pictures you may be fortunate enough to collect into two principal categories—pre-George Stubbs and post-George Stubbs. For that great artist who died in 1806 stands out like a giant, all other sporting painters seeming like pygmies when compared to his eminence.

The three most notable painters of sporting pictures in the pre-Stubbs era were Francis Barlow (1626–1704), John Wootton (1678–1765) and James Seymour (1702–1752). It is highly unlikely that any unrecorded pictures by any of these men remain for the modern collector to discover, but they were in a sense the founder-figures of this specially English school, and their work is well worth studying if you have a chance to see any examples.

Francis Barlow was born and brought up in Lincolnshire, and learned his craft under a portrait painter called Shepherd, which may account for the rare exactness of his draughtsmanship.

He quickly became successful and prosperous, and was

referred to by John Evelyn as 'the famous painter of Fowle, Beasts and Birds'. In 1665 he published a translation of *Aesop's Fables* with 110 plates engraved from his own designs, and in 1687 he brought out a large etching *The Last Horse Race Run Before Charles the Second at Dorsett Ferry in 1684*, which appears to be the earliest British sporting print. His works, many of which showed sportsmen hunting, fishing or shooting, attained considerable popularity abroad.

John Wootton was considered the greatest horse painter of his day, and in consequence he received many commissions to paint racehorses of which the noble owners were particularly proud. He had two noticeable peculiarities that make his work especially memorable. The first was his intense admiration for the great classical painters of the Continent, which often led him to provide Graeco-Roman backgrounds, with columns and urns, for the bloodstock he painted at Newmarket. The second was his desire to plan his sporting (and other) pictures on a really epic scale. The great series of hunting scenes he carried out for the entrance hall at Althorp are among the largest pictures in Britain. A canvas thirty feet long, to be filled with hounds and horsemen in a charming landscape, offered Wootton the kind of challenge that he considered really worthy of his powers.

James Seymour worked on a smaller scale and in a less ambitious way, and his sincere representations of packs of foxhounds in full cry—each hound with its legs fully extended fore and aft—have a gentle naiveté that is reminiscent of the work of the Douanier Rousseau. Until the invention of the camera, most artists found it impossible to represent convincingly, in their correct relative positions, the legs of a horse seen in a canter or at the gallop. Seymour solved this problem to his own satisfaction by setting his huntsmen on stylized rocking-horses, of little truth but infinite charm, and this solution was 'borrowed' with great facility by several of Seymour's contemporaries. Seymour's most famous picture is probably *The Great Carriage Match against Time* which depicts a memorable feat carried out at Newmarket for a thousand-guinea wager. To win the bet, a four-horse carriage with four running wheels and one driver had to be made to travel for nineteen miles within an hour. The wager was won with six minutes to spare.

And then the history of sporting art was changed by the appearance of George Stubbs, who served part of an apprenticeship in the north of England. (He walked out on his master before his time was up because he objected to having to copy another painter's pictures.)

Much of the quality of Stubbs's work can be ascribed to this sturdy independence and to his ceaseless pursuit of knowledge. As far as we know, he was the first painter to study the anatomy of the horse in any great detail. As powerful as a horse himself, he is believed to have taken the carcass of a horse up to his attic with the aid only of one female servant. There he suspended the carcass from the rafters and carried out a careful dissection. This was a lengthy operation, interrupted as it was by numerous pauses while Stubbs stopped to draw the layers of muscle and sinew his knife had uncovered, and it roused the fury of Stubbs's neighbours who found the smell of the putrefying meat almost unendurable. (History does not record what Stubbs thought of the atmosphere in which he was working.) However, he suffered—if he noticed the smell at all—in a good cause, for no artist before or since has painted horses with such sublime authority. You may never be able to afford a genuine canvas by Stubbs —they fetch many hundreds of pounds—but you will enjoy studying any of his paintings that you may see in the public collections, and they may help you to discriminate between the works of the primitive but genuine horse painters of the eighteenth century, the masterpieces produced in the early nineteenth century, and the slushy studio contrivances of the late Victorian 'decadents' who cared only for popular appeal.

In 1766 Stubbs published his monumental work *The Anatomy of the Horse*. The drawings alone had taken him eighteen months of unremitting labour: then, undeterred by his failure to find an engraver competent enough (and willing enough) to undertake such a colossal task, he learned how to wield a burin himself and spent all his spare time during the next six or seven years transferring his drawings on to plates.

The work brought him an international reputation. As one
critic said:

> *'The wide Creation waits upon his call,*
> *He paints each species and excels in all,*
> *Whilst wondering Nature asks with jealous Tone,*
> *Which Stubbs's labours are and which her own.'*

Not surprisingly, Stubbs's work had a great influence on
the sporting artists of his time, and in no painter's work can
this be seen more noticeably than in the austere canvases of
Benjamin Marshall (1767–1835). Marshall was almost as
keen a student of equine anatomy as the great man himself,
and his pictures of horses were drawn and painted with an
earnest integrity that must have been highly satisfying to the
knowledgeable patrons who commissioned them. To many
modern eyes, however, Marshall's canvases lack warmth, life
and charm, and the work of his pupil John Ferneley (1782–
1860) is more highly regarded. Certainly, the set of engravings made from Ferneley's stirring paintings of 'Count
Sandor's Hunting Exploits in Leicestershire' can still cause
plenty of amusement, even though the full significance of the
Count's solecisms and the finer points of the misadventures
he suffered may be thrown away on the twentieth-century
spectator.

The animal studies of James Ward (1769–1859) are also
full of vigorous movement, and they are as popular today as
they have ever been. It would be stretching a point to call
most of them 'sporting pictures', for Ward was happiest
when he was depicting bulls fighting with horses, bulls fighting with bulls, horses fighting with horses, horses fighting
with snakes, or any other combination of these or similar
antagonists. Usually, Ward would arrange for these struggles
to take place when a change in the weather was imminent,
and in settings of considerable grandeur—he even managed
to give a certain lonely magnificence to Marylebone Fields.

Ward is believed to have retired from London when he
was sixty-one and to have spent the last thirty years of his
life in an obscure country retreat. He is known to have produced many more paintings than are at present accounted

for. It might be a profitable occupation, therefore, for a collector to become thoroughly familiar with his style.

In the reigns of George III, George IV and 'Pineapple' William, the demand for sporting paintings and prints was so great that whole families made good livings by helping to swell the supply. It is important for the collector of sporting pictures to know something about these families and their individual members, for the percipient searcher is much more likely to pick up (say) an unrecognized Herring or a Sartorius at a reasonable price than he is to find a cheap Barlow, an unwanted Marshall, or an unrecorded but genuine Stubbs. It would not be easy to arrange these families in chronological order, for in some cases their members followed the calling for several decades. Here, then, is a brief description of some of the most important families of 'sporting' artists, arranged alphabetically:

The *Alkens*. It is fitting that the Alkens, who were of Scandinavian origin, should come first in the list, for Henry Alken (1785–1851) was outstandingly successful at depicting scenes in the English hunting field, having a splendid feeling for extensive landscapes, and the ability to convey some of the excitements of the chase. Among his most famous pictures are *The Night Riders of Nacton* in which Alken showed some Ipswich cavalry officers riding a steeplechase in their night-shirts, *A Spree at Melton Mowbray* which shows the notorious John Mytton and a bunch of his cronies literally painting that sedate old town red, and a study, which was later issued as a popular print, of Squire Osbaldeston's Two Hundred Miles Race against Time. Other members of the family who made sporting art their profession were Henry's father Samuel Alken (1750–1815), his brother Samuel Alken Junior (1784–1825) and his son Henry Gordon Alken (1810–1892). For some reason, Henry Alken signed his early pictures with the pseudonym 'Ben Tally O'.

In the *Herring* family the outstanding figure is undoubtedly the patriarchal J. F. Herring (1795–1865) whose pictures have always been popular with connoisseurs and amateur collectors alike. Herring started his career as a stage-coach driver. Then he started to paint inn signs in his spare time.

Showing a remarkable facility, he was taken up and given a thorough training by one Abraham Cooper, a specialist in battle pictures. Herring quickly found more patrons including, unfortunately, Queen Victoria, who gave him a horse that had been presented to her by the Sultan of Arabia, and this poor old expatriate beast tends to reappear with monotonous regularity in many of Herring's later pictures. Herring's work is of especial interest to the owners and breeders of racehorses because he made exact likenesses of so many famous winners, including all the winners of the St Leger Stakes for thirty-five successive years. His sons Ben Herring and Charles Herring followed in their father's footsteps, but without anything like his success.

The *Pollard* family are next on our list. Robert Pollard (1758–1838) moved to London from Newcastle, took lessons from Richard Wilson, and then set himself up in business as a printer and publisher of sporting pictures, finding it particularly profitable to specialize in coaching and racing scenes. He was helped by his son James, who was particularly good at depicting the exciting vicissitudes that sometimes befell the well organized stage-coach services, and who also painted and engraved some memorable incidents in contemporary steeplechases. Pollard prints are not hard to find, and (for their quality) are relatively inexpensive.

The *Sartorius* family seems to have spanned four generations, the eldest member John Sartorius having come originally from Bavaria. This John was the father of Francis Sartorius (born 1734), the grandfather of John Nort Sartorius (*c.* 1753–1828) and the great-grandfather of John F. Sartorius. Only experts can tell the Sartorius' work apart without looking for the signatures, but all, from the 'primitive' studies of Francis to the graceful landscapes of John N. have an undeniable appeal.

The *Wolstenholmes* became professional artists after a series of family misfortunes. Dean Wolstenholme Senior (1757–1837) was a Yorkshire gentleman of means who enjoyed drawing and painting when he was not indulging in the outdoor pursuits considered appropriate at that time to a person of his estate. After a succession of lawsuits had whittled away his fortune, Wolstenholme decided to restore his financial position by commercializing his talents and his intimate knowledge of the life of the countryside. His paintings, many of which had such graphic titles as *Reynard Seeks Refuge in the Church*, and the engravings that were made from them had an immediate popular success. Dean Wolstenholme Junior (1798–1882) continued the good work started by his father.

When the demand for sporting pictures lessened, midway through Queen Victoria's reign, the standards set by purveyors of 'field art' became noticeably less consistent. Since that time there have been a few really good artists who have been attracted to sporting subjects from personal inclination, and a great many more whose talents have been as limited as their knowledge of a sportsman's equipment and outdoor etiquette. It would be tedious (and possibly libellous) to make a list of the modern sporting artists whose work would seem flimsy or pretentious when placed against a Marshall or a Stubbs, but there are three controversial figures from the intervening years who must not be omitted.

The first of these is Sir Edwin Landseer, RA (1802–1873), whose works were 'best sellers' when the novels of Trollope and Scott were booming. There were few middle-class homes at the end of the nineteenth century without at least one reproduction of a Landseer stag or a Landseer St Bernard on the walls, and the really great houses even boasted a wall of Landseer originals. The secret of his popular appeal is not hard to understand—he was a sensitive and competent artist who learned, too young, the trick of endowing dumb animals with human feelings. A painting of a Scottish crofter's dogs mourning their prematurely deceased master could be guaranteed to bring tears to any soft-hearted matron's eyes, and most Victorian matrons whose husbands were in the correct income group were ready to see large sums put down to procure for them that delectable experience. Nowadays our pleasures are a little more complex, and most of Landseer's tear-jerkers have been relegated, with some embarrassment, to a store-room, a guests' bedroom or an unfrequented passage.

The second artist, whose sporting pictures have deservedly kept their popularity, is Lionel Edwards. His huntsmen may not be as anatomically convincing as Landseer's ghillies and his horses may be dashed in with a bravura that blinds us to their sketchy conformation, but the landscapes in which the artist sets them are delightful evocations of hunting country under varying conditions of wind, rain and rare bursts of sunshine. It might not be an exaggeration to call Lionel Edwards a major English Impressionist, with sporting preoccupations.

The third is, of course, Sir Alfred Munnings, PRA (1878–1959). Opinions differ about the merits of Munnings' work —some observers are more irritated than impressed by the artist's fluent virtuosity, by his frequent indifference to scale and by the superficiality of his rendering of form, but there is no doubt that his paintings offer to many people's eyes a last sad reminder of the Golden Age of the horse.

Clearly, the list of sporting artists included in this chapter cannot be regarded as comprehensive, or anything like it. In a longer book there would probably be space for more than a brief passing mention of Sawrey Gilpin (1733–1807), recorder of racehorses in a particularly pleasing way; Philip Reinagle (1749–1833), whose major works included *The Sportsman's Cabinet*—a popular series of pictures of sporting dogs; Samuel Howitt (1765–1822), who was Rowlandson's brother-in-law and who contributed many excellent hunting and shooting pictures to *Orme's Collection of British Field Sports and Oriental Field Sports*; Charles Cooper Henderson (1803–1877) who caught in his pictures all the bustle and excitement of the great days of coaching; and, more recently, Ivestor Lloyd, who specialized in pictures of beagles and beagling, and Peter Scott, whose studies of wildfowl, backed by his encyclopaedic knowledge of the subject, have earned him an international reputation. Enough names have been quoted to show that the field open to the collector of sporting pictures is an exceptionally wide one. Even the sports that have become popular in comparatively recent times, such as skiing, motor racing and professional boxing, are now being looked at by artists as fruitful sources of subject-matter.

11

CLEANING AND RESTORING

THE BEST advice anyone can give to an amateur picture collector who would like to give a new lease of life to a picture without expert help is the same advice as Mr Punch would give to a young man about to marry: 'Don't!' As Hilaire Hiler puts it in his excellent book *Notes on the Technique of Painting* published by Messrs Faber & Faber: 'It is a peculiar characteristic of many human natures that they are hypnotically carried on in any operations which have to do with cleaning, brightening or polishing. Once started in on these operations, only sudden death can stop them.' In the process of 'restoration', an unskilled person may do irremediable damage to the fabric of the picture on which he or she is operating. This can be serious if the picture has any appreciable market value.

There are, however, certain steps that can be safely taken to keep the pictures in a collection in ship-shape order. It is impossible to go into this complicated subject in great detail in a chapter as short as this has to be, but the information given in the next few pages, brief as it is, may enable you to take a more balanced view of fine art conservation.

CLEANING OIL-PAINTINGS

An old, dirty oil-painting may cry out for a face-lift, so that its colours may be seen in all their pristine brilliance, but a scrubbing with soap and water is not a treatment that any chemist would recommend. The water is liable to penetrate any cracks there may be in the oil film, so that it softens the glue-bound ground beneath, and soap and other alkalis can be definitely harmful. There are safer methods.

The best alternative is undoubtedly to give the surface of the painting a light rub with a piece of cloth that has been moistened (no more) with clean petrol or lighter fuel. As soon as the cloth becomes dirty it should be thrown away and a fresh piece should be taken. Cotton wool is sometimes recommended as it is so very soft, but it has a distinct tendency to leave white whiskers behind wherever the paint surface has roughness or 'tooth'.

Other cleaning substances beside petrol are sometimes prescribed by authorities who have developed techniques that do not appear to have any immediately harmful effects. Turpentine and alcohol have been freely used in the past, but both these have a tendency to soften varnish, and their action may be disastrous if they are not used with the utmost discretion. Raw potato and bread are rudimentary cleansers but cannot be recommended. More questionable still is the expedient described in the magazine *Cosmos* in the last decade of the nineteenth century under the title 'Cleaning of Old Pictures by Dr Alb. Battandier's Method':

'To clean an old picture without damaging the paint, Dr. Battandier counsels using neither acids, which, he says, eat the colours and remove the delicate gradations or glazes, nor alkalis and soap . . . He declares himself in favour of a liquid which anyone may easily procure, and which, if its handling is not exactly as attractive as it might be, has nevertheless a precious result.

'This liquid is urine, as far as possible freshly vented, and at its normal temperature, that is to say, about 35° C., with which the painting should be washed. This liquid softens foreign bodies adhering to the surface to be cleaned, such as smoke, dust, fly-specks, etc., and it is removed afterwards easily by rubbing with a little flexible stick of soft wood, taking care not to scratch the painting.

'Two or three washings suffice to remove the varnish from the picture, together with any dirt which is soiling its surface. In the case of small pictures of only a few square centimetres, which, it is true, form a case quite rarely met with, saliva may be substituted for the urine.'

After reading that, you will probably decide to stick to petrol.

REMOVING BLOOM FROM OIL-PAINTINGS

'Bloom' is the name given to an unpleasant white mist that sometimes disfigures varnished oil-paintings. It frequently results when one of the soft resin varnishes has been used under unsuitable conditions—as, for example, when the underlying painting has not been left to 'dry' long enough before the varnish has been applied, or when the varnishing has been done on a damp or rainy day.

Normally, bloom can be removed fairly easily. Try, first, rubbing an affected picture with a silk handkerchief. If that does not do the trick, put one drop of turpentine and one drop of linseed oil together in a teaspoon and let them mingle. Then pick up a trace of the resulting fluid on a clean cloth and rub it lightly over the surface of the picture. Wipe all traces of this away, if it proves effective, or the picture will quickly become unpleasantly sticky.

DEALING WITH CRACKS IN OIL-PAINTINGS

That is rather an optimistic heading, for any crack in a paint film is a symptom of damage that only an expert picture restorer can hope to repair. You will probably be able to prevent further deterioration, though, if you can trace the cause or causes of the damage that has been done already.

Paintings that have been carried out on canvas will obviously be more prone to damage by violence of various kinds than paintings on wood or board panels. A paint film that has suffered a blow, or that has been strained by having the corner of another picture pressed against it, will often show cracks like concentric rings round the seat of the trouble.

A coat of paint that is placed over an unprimed ground or a ground that is too absorbent will probably lose a lot of its binding fluid and with it its elasticity. Fine irregular cracks that look like the 'crazing' of an old china glaze will almost certainly develop under these conditions.

A coat of paint that has been applied to another coat before the underlying surface is quite dry and inert is almost certain to crack. So is a coat of paint in which the vehicle has been unevenly distributed (this is especially true of a paint skin in which a varnish medium has been incorporated without due regard for consistency).

Old pictures that were painted by artists who wished to achieve rich, dark effects quickly often contain traces of bitumen. This was a mineral pitch—it is thoroughly discredited nowadays—that has probably done more damage to paintings, over the years, than any other single cause except loss by fire. The trouble is caused by bitumen's failure to dry or harden, even after a period of years. Imagine locking away a layer of liquid tar inside a film of paint and you will see why a picture that looks as if it may have been painted with bitumen is not to be recommended as an investment.

You will probably do more damage by attempting to fill fine cracks in your oil-paintings, or in attempting to make them invisible, than the operation is worth. Some restorers will hold a cracked painting upside down over a bath of alcohol so that the fumes may have a softening effect, but it is easy to see that this procedure may be perilous, to say the least. A safer expedient (if you really want to experiment with a picture that is never likely to go to a top saleroom) is to give the cracked area a light dressing of retouching varnish.

MENDING A TORN CANVAS

Cracks in an oil-paint film are rarely so noticeable that they interfere completely with our enjoyment of a picture. Even a small hole or tear in a canvas may be such an obvious blemish that it makes an appreciative scrutiny impossible.

If a picture with a hole or tear is valuable, or likely to become so, repair work should only be done by an expert, but there is no reason why you should not put an invisible patch, which will also act as a reinforcement, on any run-of-the-mill oil-painting in your collection that may have met with a mishap.

First, find a flat hard surface to work on (plate glass or marble will be ideal).

Then put the canvas face down on this, with a thin piece of paper that you have previously moistened with petrol or lighter fuel underneath the section that needs a repair.

Then take a warm (not hot) flat iron and press the torn edges of the canvas gently together, or as close as may be possible.

Then stick a patch of paper over the whole area to be repaired, using a good quality casein glue as the adhesive, and using the flat iron again to press the patch perfectly flat.

Then stick a canvas patch over the back of the paper patch, but make it slightly smaller than the original reinforcement so that the edges of the paper are visible all round. Again, use the flat iron to make the canvas patch perfectly flat.

Finish by giving the whole area of the repair a few coats of retouching varnish, leaving each coat to dry out thoroughly before you add the next. If you carry the varnish over the edges of the reinforcement and let it soak well into the original canvas it will help to keep the edges of the patch from curling away.

Then turn the picture over, fill the cracks with zinc white or a little Polyfilla, and when this has dried out thoroughly touch up the surface with colour so that it merges as far as possible into the original paint surface.

RE-LINING

This is an operation that is sometimes carried out when the canvas on which a valuable picture has been painted deteriorates to a degree at which it no longer affords the paint surface adequate support. The operation is a lengthy one and should only be carried out by experienced professional craftsmen. As it is expensive, it is usually reserved for works of art that are really worth cherishing.

First, the picture is cleaned and then a sheet of strong paper is pasted over the face of it, a water soluble paste (usually a flour paste) being used as the adhesive.

Then the canvas is removed from its stretcher and pinned face down on a wooden table or some other perfectly flat working surface.

Next comes the most difficult part of the operation—the removal of the rotten canvas completely (this is done in extreme cases) so that a new canvas can be applied to the reverse side of the ground or (more generally) so that the new canvas can be applied to the back of the old canvas, the two being united with the best quality size and glue. As warm irons are used by professional restorers at this stage of the operation, it will be seen that a considerable amount of self-confidence is called for, as well as skill.

When all the adhesives used are thoroughly dry, the canvas is removed from the working surface, the paper that has been protecting the paint film is soaked away, and the picture is dried, re-stretched and sometimes re-varnished.

It would be improper to leave the subject of the conservation and restoration of pictures without emphasizing again most forcibly the dangers of unskilled treatment. Irreparable damage may be done to a picture by the well-meaning amateur. If any of the pictures in your collection have any real quality or possible value do, please, seek expert advice rather than try treating them yourself.

12

FAKES AND FORGERIES

EVERYONE who invests money in a picture—or in any work of art that is not purchased directly from the man who created it—will be interested in the mental processes and the technical methods of the faker and forger. The relationship between the collector and the manufacturer of spurious masterpieces is not unlike that between two adversaries who are engaged in an unceasing guerrilla struggle. As long as you collect pictures solely for pleasure, the conflict will probably cause you mild amusement. As soon as your collection starts to become really valuable, you will be more concerned to see that all your accessions really are genuine, and you will almost certainly develop a mild interest at least in the processes by which art experts divide the authentic from the spurious—or how they attempt to!

Unfortunately for the commercially-minded collector, there is no such thing as an absolutely incontrovertible Certificate of Genuineness that can be given with one hundred per cent certainty to any work of art unless its provenance or previous history can be traced and vouched for, without one single missing link in the chain, from the moment that it first left the artist's workroom. Before one can begin to appreciate even a small proportion of the complexities of the matter, one has to be aware of the subtle distinctions that are drawn by experts between 'forgeries'—that is, works of art that are entirely spurious, and have been deliberately produced to deceive; 'fakes'—that is, works that are partly genuine, but have been altered or added to in order to increase their market value; and the 'replicas' of various kinds that have been made with no ulterior motive. Each category calls for closer examination.

Let us begin, first, with the completely genuine work of

art. To qualify for this desirable verdict, a picture will have had to be produced, right from the earliest sketches to the last finishing touches, by the hand of the artist to whom it is attributed. Modern paintings are rarely produced by team-work methods, and are fairly certain to be either completely genuine or forged, but works that date from the eighteenth century and earlier are much more difficult to certify. Then, most artists of any repute would have a number of pupils and paid assistants working in their studios, and these men would be expected to carry out most of the more menial tasks associated with painting—the learners would be given various elementary jobs to do, such as laying grounds and burnishing them, and transferring the outlines of cartoons; the skilled men might specialize in painting hands, or drapery, or backgrounds: much of the artist's time would be spent in receiving clients and entertaining them, in accepting or rejecting their commissions, and in extracting payment. If he were a conscientious artist, and not too busy handling the commercial side of his venture, he would work over the whole surface of a canvas himself, at least once, before it left his studio. If he was too successful to have any time for this, he might be content with giving the picture a thorough appraisal, adding a few touches where the drawing seemed weak, recommending an extra glaze or two, and putting his signature or monogram in one corner to show that it went out with his approval. After the lapse of several hundred years it takes a very clever man to tell just where the work of a master finished and that of his staff began—or the other way about!

In extreme cases, a painting might reach the patron who had commissioned it without getting more than a cursory glance from the Master. An order for a royal portrait, for example, might be accompanied by an order for a dozen or more replicas, each of which would be intended for some embassy or government building overseas. When an expert suspects that a picture falls into this category he will usually assign it to the 'Studio of X', or he will pronounce it to be 'In the style of Y'. The presence of a signature or monogram on such a printing does not mean that the expert is being over-cautious.

9

Besides these replicas made in an artist's studio which bear the authority of the Master if not his genuine autograph, the collector has other copies to bear in mind, notably those made by lesser artists, without authority, and often in a travesty of the original style. Obviously the more popular an artist's work becomes, and the higher the prices it commands, the more likely it is to attract the attentions of the copyists. There is a well-known (and frequently varied) saying in the art world to the effect that Corot painted two thousand pictures, of which at least nine thousand are in America!

As the work of the unauthorized copyist presents so many problems to the picture collector, it will be as well, if you are lucky enough to own any pictures that you think may be valuable, to study this aspect of art-dilution, as the experts do, in considerable detail.

First, it is important to bear in mind the difference between a 'contemporary' copy—that is, one made during the life-time of the artist responsible for the original—and a copy made after a considerable lapse of time.

A contemporary copy may well be much more difficult to spot than a copy made in a subsequent generation, because the copyist will almost certainly have had access to the same kinds of materials as the artist who produced the original. An expert examining an oil-painting will look closely for certain tell-tale signs:

He will scrutinize the panel on which the picture is painted, or the stretcher to which the canvas is pinned. Obviously, whichever has been used, the wood should be of a kind that was available, and favoured by artists, at the time when the picture was 'officially' painted. A stretcher, too, should be of the right type to be even moderately convincing—the fact that no tongued and grooved stretchers were used before the nineteenth century is sometimes worth remembering. But no tests on a support can really be conclusive because an astute forger will often obtain an indifferent painting of the correct period so that he can remove the paint film and replace it with his own! Occasionally, too, an old and quite genuine canvas will be found to have been taken off its original frame during some restoration and re-stretched on a modern one.

Clearly this does not invalidate that painting in the slightest degree, but it is a good idea, if you encounter this, to check that you can see in the borders of the canvas the original tack-holes or nail-holes.

The age of the canvas itself can be assessed by an expert with a fair degree of accuracy, because he will have become accustomed from long experience to the look and the feel of the fabrics produced in the various periods. Until the Industrial Revolution, all canvases were woven by hand. If you once study a genuine eighteenth-century canvas carefully and compare it with a modern machine-woven canvas you should subsequently be able to tell the difference without much difficulty.

After he has studied the support and the ground (if any is visible) the expert will probably turn his attention to the paint film, and here he will be in a much stronger position than the amateur, who has only rarely the facilities needed for subjecting small particles of material to chemical or spectroscopic analysis. Among the pigments which may help the expert to 'date' a picture are artificial ultramarine, which was first prepared by a Frenchman named Guimet in 1824 and which quickly replaced the rare and expensive real colour, made from lapis lazuli; cobalt blue, which was not used by artists before 1802; the cadmiums and the chrome oxide colours, developed at intervals during the early nineteenth century; and the powerful Prussian blue which was first produced by the German chemist Diesbach in 1704. The presence of any of these colours in a picture supposed to have been painted before that colour was introduced may usually be taken as conclusive evidence of malpractice.

In examining closely the various parts of a painting, the expert will become aware of certain characteristics that pertain to the whole of it, and this is something that even an absolute novice can learn to do.

He will be conscious of the general maturity of the paint surface, as the forger finds it quite difficult to produce with colours that are fresh from the tube a paint film that looks and feels two hundred or three hundred years old. The older an oil-paint film becomes, the harder it will tend to be—for the first year or two it can be scratched easily with a pin, but this is not a test that can be recommended, for obvious reasons, if the scratch is likely to do several hundreds of pounds' worth of damage. Sometimes a forger will hasten the hardening process by heating a picture in an oven, so no rudimentary hardness test is really infallible.

Then, the expert will have a close look at the minute cracks with which the paint film (if it is an old one) is virtually certain to be marked. In a forged picture, these will have had to be produced by some artificial means—rolling a canvas tightly round a broom handle is one rough-and-ready method —but the difference between a genuine crack (that is, one produced by the slow movement, over many decades, of successive layers of paint and varnish) and a crack produced in a fairly new paint film by tension or fracture is usually fairly apparent if an enlarged photograph, taken under suitably strong oblique lighting, is carefully studied.

In forming an opinion about the authenticity (or otherwise) of any painting that purports to be more than a few years old, an expert may be helped by any knowledge he may have acquired of the dress and furniture fashionable in the period in which the picture is supposed to have originated. Clearly, a genuine picture will contain no details of costume, jewellery, coiffure, make-up, armour, saddlery, stance, gesture or interior decoration that are in any way anachronistic. It would be virtually impossible for a forger to be an authority in all these extensive fields. So, it is highly likely that a forged picture, unless it is a photographically exact replica of a genuine one, will contain some inexact feature, omission or distortion that reveals its spurious origins—an early Victorian teapot included in an 'eighteenth-century' conversation piece, for example, might not be noticed by the average picture collector, but it would sound an unmistakable warning note to anyone who had a detailed knowledge of porcelain and tableware. To be well-informed in picture-collecting is to be forearmed.

The fourth—and possibly the most important—factor the forgery-hunter has to bear in mind is the personal style of the artist whose work he is studying. This is a particularly subtle matter, since it may depend on idiosyncrasies of handling and brushwork that the artist himself might have been unable to discern. Only a prolonged study of the best, well authenticated work of any master will give a collector the strange 'sixth sense' or instinct that cannot be bought, taught or acquired from books. Great art historians such as Bernhard Berenson and Dr Wilhelm von Bode have become known all over the world (and have earned sumptuous livings in the process) by developing this authoritative judgement, but even these famous experts have not always found it easy to justify their decisions. The former actually said, when he was being cross-examined in a famous court case: 'When I see a picture in most cases I recognize it at once as being or not being by the master it is ascribed to; the rest is merely a question of how to fish out the evidence that will make the conviction as plain to others as it is to me.'

No chapter on forged and faked pictures would be complete without some reference to the great Wacker scandal, and to that fantastic person Han van Meegeren, whose activities aroused extraordinary interest in the years following the Second World War.

The well-documented frauds with which the dealer Otto Wacker was associated were first brought to the notice of the art trade, the police and the public by the celebrated French critic and art expert Dr J. B. de la Faille. In 1927 de la Faille published a list of all the known works by Vincent Van Gogh, the strange Dutch Post-Impressionist who had died nearly forty years before. In compiling his catalogue, de la Faille had been helped by the letters Van Gogh had written to his brother Theo describing his work, by the records made by Theo when he received the genuine canvases, and by Otto Wacker.

In 1928 an exhibition of Van Gogh's work was mounted at the Galerie Paul Cassirer, in the Viktoriastrasse in Berlin. To this exhibition Wacker, who had his gallery in the same street, contributed four canvases. As they moved around the works they had assembled, the proprietors of the Galerie Paul Cassirer found that the 'sixth sense' to which we have already referred was causing them acute disquiet. The four canvases

contributed by Otto Wacker seemed, on close inspection, to
be inharmonious with the others and slightly out of style.
So they sent them back to Wacker unexhibited.

When this came to the ears of Dr de la Faille, who had
become by that time the recognized authority on the work of
Van Gogh, he acted quickly. Without at first committing
himself publicly, he set himself the task of re-examining
meticulously every one of the Van Gogh canvases which could
possibly be considered 'doubtful'. All, he found, had come on
to the market in ones and twos (never in larger quantities)
and all had come from the establishment of Otto Wacker.

Wacker's story was a colourful one. He claimed that he had
obtained the paintings from a Russian nobleman who was
living in Switzerland. Pressed to reveal the identity of this
collector, Wacker refused on the grounds that his client was
a refugee, that he had sworn to keep his identity secret, and
that the lives of the members of his family who were still in
Russia would be endangered by any publicity.

Dr de la Faille was not to be so easily shrugged off. By a
masterly piece of scholarship he built up an unanswerable case
against Wacker. Then, fully confident of his ground, he
brought out a supplement to the catalogue he had originally
published, listing in it all the 'Van Gogh' paintings he definitely considered to be spurious, and including in his list of
forgeries a few canvases that he had previously vouched for
as genuine. De la Faille's researches culminated in the arrest,
trial, and imprisonment of Otto Wacker—a sequence of events
which shook the confidence of many picture collectors and
put a brake, momentarily, on the rapidly rising price spiral
of the principal Post-Impressionists.

Fifteen years after Otto Wacker was sentenced, the case of
Han van Meegeren claimed world-wide attention. In fact, it
would hardly be an exaggeration to say that van Meegeren
was the most famous picture forger there has ever been or is
ever likely to be.

The facts of van Meegeren's life are fairly well known.
Born in 1889, he was the son of a stern Dutch schoolmaster
who had little sympathy with his youthful attempts to become
an artist. Instead of being allowed to follow his inclinations,

the boy was sent to Delft to study for a more 'respectable' career as an architect. The boy's private ambitions won, and in 1914 he was awarded a gold medal and a large money fee in a painting competition held by The Hague Academy.

Van Meegeren had been married twice, and was supporting two children, before the idea of painting a masterpiece in the style of one of the most famous old painters took root in his mind. His motives seem to have been more complex than those of Otto Wacker—the pleasure he expected to get from outwitting the experts and authorities was, he declared later, just as tempting as the probable financial reward.

Van Meegeren's first aim was to paint a false Vermeer, which was to be called *The Disciples in Emmaus*. It is easy to see why van Meegeren picked on Vermeer as the subject of his attentions. Not only was the great man closely associated with Delft, where van Meegeren had studied, but, also, the circumstances of the artist's life were conveniently shrouded in mystery. It was known that he had died in his prime in 1675, leaving eight children, that he had spent most of his life in penury, and that he had never, while he was still working, been considered as a master. During the eighteenth century his paintings were little appreciated, and during the first decades of the nineteenth century his name was virtually forgotten. It was only when the great art critic Thoré-Bürger visited The Hague Museum in 1842 and recognized his genius that Vermeer's true worth was acclaimed. If such a neglected man had produced some forgotten masterpieces would it be so very surprising?

Van Meegeren went to extraordinary lengths to acquire the esoteric skills necessary for his dishonest enterprise, travelling great distances to study Vermeer's few authentic masterpieces, reading everything that had ever been written about the artist's techniques, experimenting with all kinds of old paints and essences, and purchasing as many seventeenth-century household utensils for use as 'properties' as he could find and afford. By the time he was ready to embark on his great enterprise, he felt so confident of his technical prowess that he was prepared to spend several weeks rubbing the paint gently from a genuine but indifferent *Raising of Lazarus*, the work of a contemporary of Vermeer, so that he could use the old canvas as a base.

It took van Meegeren six months to complete his first major forgery. He made brushes especially from badger-hair shaving brushes, as he knew that one single bristle that looked unfamiliar to the experts who would be certain to scrutinize a newly found masterpiece would make the whole deception immediately apparent. He found an anonymous nomad to pose as a model for the 'Christ' figure in the picture, as he knew that professional models might talk. He discovered a method of hardening his pigments by mixing them with phenol and formaldehyde immediately before he applied them to the canvas. He produced a fine network of cracks in the finished picture by a careful process of rolling and baking. During the whole of this time, the van Meegeren household was servant-less. The master wanted no inquisitive eyes prying into the secrets of his workshop.

When the picture was finished, van Meegeren took it to Paris. There, he offered it discreetly to a dealer, pretending that it belonged to a noble but impoverished Italian family who were determined, for reasons of pride, to remain un-identified, and that he, van Meegeren, was acting simply as a go-between. The dealer swallowed the bait with a rush. What dealer would not, when the picture he was being offered looked so extremely convincing?

The remarkable thing is, that even the acknowledged experts who were then invited to submit the picture to the most rigorous tests were fooled, too. They tried rubbing the outer surface with alcohol, only to find that van Meegeren's carefully doctored paint film did not immediately dissolve. They bombarded the picture with X-rays, but these did not reveal anything untoward—van Meegeren had been too care-ful to leave any traces of the 'Lazarus', visible or invisible. They removed tiny particles of each of the main pigments van Meegeren had used and submitted them to the customary microscopic and spectroscopic surveys. These, too, showed nothing suspicious—van Meegeren had even imported real lapis lazuli, for preparing the true ultramarine he needed, from as far away as London. So the experts' verdict was unanimous: a real and previously unknown Vermeer had come to light in the middle of the twentieth century!

In considering the later stages of van Meegeren's fantastic career, and in asking ourselves how the man dared, having been so amazingly successful at his first attempt, to repeat his audacious experiments, or variations on them, not once, not twice, but at least nine known times, we have to remember that he was living at a particularly propitious moment in history for the picture forger, when frontiers were closed and communication between the great art centres of the world was temporarily in abeyance. It is pleasantly ironic that van Meegeren should have been compelled to confess to his activities as a forger in order to clear himself of the far greater crime of collaborating with Holland's erstwhile enemies.

The final *dénouement* in the van Meegeren affair came just after the cessation of hostilities in 1945. Then, when the members of one of the Commissions sent by the victorious Allies to examine the art treasures plundered by the Nazis and their associates were looking at the pictures and other works of art accumulated by Hermann Goering, the Dutch members of the Commission noticed a painting, apparently by Vermeer, that none of them remembered having seen anywhere before. Immediately an investigation was started into the picture's past history, for it would have been against Dutch law for any unauthorized person to export a Vermeer at all, and the crime would have been infinitely worse if the picture, wherever it came from, had been handed over to the Germans deliberately by a traitor. Soon the picture was traced back to van Meegeren, and the Dutchman was arrested. Knowing that it would be fruitless to try to deny any knowledge of the picture, and knowing, too, that he could be all too easily accused of treachery, van Meegeren signed a full confession of his misdeeds. How, he argued, could anyone be convicted of collaboration if all he had done was to succeed in deceiving a gullible enemy?

It was a nice point, but it saved van Meegeren from life imprisonment. He was given a shorter sentence, but his health failed while he was serving it, and he died, still the centre of a storm of publicity, on the thirtieth day of December, 1947.

13

WINDFALLS

ONE DAY when the sculptor Jacques Lipchitz was passing the window of a New York sale room, he noticed, among a pile of second-hand furniture that was awaiting disposal, a print that took his fancy. When he went inside and inquired about the print he was told that it was to be included in a sale to be held some days later. He was told, too, that he could put down a deposit if he wished, and that this would secure the lot if no higher bid were received at the forthcoming auction. Lipchitz, having an eye for a good print, put down five dollars. At the sale, the print was knocked down to him for four.

At this point in the story, it seems opportune to reveal that the print was, in fact, of exceptional quality. It had survived, in excellent condition, from the fifteenth century, and was the work of Martin Schongauer. To appreciate the full significance of Lipchitz' find, one has to know that Schongauer was a very considerable artist indeed who exerted a powerful influence on his contemporaries, and whose work may be said, without exaggeration, to have made possible the later achievements of Albrecht Dürer. Even the great Michelangelo was not too proud to make a copy of a print by Schongauer, while Raphael Santi is known to have 'borrowed' from one of Schongauer's engravings the main elements of one of his most famous compositions. Lipchitz had bought, to put it mildly, a very satisfactory four dollars' worth.

The possibility of making a find like that—or, better, a whole series of such finds—is never far from the mind of most picture collectors. Stories of the El Greco panel that was bought for the odd shilling in an East London street market, of the Delacroix oil that hung unrecognized on the wall of a house in Cheltenham for at least forty years, of the

Gainsborough that changed hands for a pound only help to raise the blood pressure of a legion of crypto-Berensons. Do their pulses go racing in vain?

The answer to that question is probably 'yes', though there is a million to one chance that any collector may be as lucky as Lipchitz. 'As *lucky* as Lipchitz?' one can almost hear the experienced picture-shopper echoing. 'That certainly is the wrong word.' Perhaps it is. You need more than good fortune to pick up a Schongauer, or an El Greco, or a Delacroix, or a Gainsborough.

First, you have to be hunting in the right place, and that means just about everywhere, unlikely as well as likely. There are certain hunting-grounds that have earned through long decades the reputation of being the right places to look—the 'Flea Market' in Paris is one of these, and the Portobello Road in London is another—but these and similar traditional searching places are so regularly and thoroughly picked over by the trade that it seems almost a waste of time for the amateur to go to them, except for a little mild interest and amusement.

Then, there are antique shops where one has a slightly better chance of finding an overlooked masterpiece. Shops with Sheraton sideboards and eighteenth-century marquetry commodes in the windows will not necessarily be any less fruitful than more modest establishments, where stuffed birds and Victoriana are the stock-in-trade. In antique shops of all grades, any picture that looks as if it has the faintest chance of being valuable will be given a very close inspection before it is offered to the public. To pick up a bargain, one has to find the occasional work that betrays a rare gap in the dealer's knowledge. The man who is an expert on ormolu-mounted *ébenisterie* may not be any more familiar with—say —the prints of Utamaro than is his neighbour next door in the newspaper shop.

The small town junk shop offers better opportunities than any antique shop—the kind that may have a top hat, a broken typewriter and some useless tennis rackets in its window, as well as a lot of old clothes, being especially promising. But even at an establishment of this kind, the casual customer may only be getting 'second refusal'—the proprietor may well have an arrangement with a dealer in a nearby city whereby the dealer is allowed a daily or weekly visit to have a first look at newly bought-in stock. Usually it is safe to say that the dowdier such a shop is, the less chance there is of its being regularly and professionally 'combed'.

The best chance of all is provided by the house clear-out, and the jumble sale. In scores of homes in this and other countries there is a spare room, attic or cupboard in which outmoded furniture, unwanted belongings and broken fittings that are to be mended 'sometime' are put away out of sight and half out of mind. Included in those rarely disturbed hoards there are thousands of pictures of all kinds that were banished because they had been in view for too long, were unfashionable, or did not fit in with a new decorative scheme. To have the opportunity of looking over a hoard of this kind before it is broken up or dispersed is an experience that any keen picture collector would find agreeable. The next best thing, of course, is to be 'first there' at a jumble sale.

In all this searching and picking over, there is one factor that must not be underestimated—the amount of study that has to be done, and the amount of knowledge that has to be acquired, if a worthy work of art is to be recognized with certainty as soon as it turns up in an unexpected place. Bernhard Berenson was not born with his extraordinary knowledge of Italian paintings of the fourteenth and fifteenth centuries—he became as familiar with them as anyone ever has been, or, probably, as anyone ever will be, by seizing every chance to look at works both major and minor in his chosen field, and by reading everything he possibly could about their history. As a result he would probably have been able to spot an unrecorded Filippo Lippi, towards the end of his life, on one of the stalls if he had driven past a crowded market-place in a swiftly moving car. Anyone who is prepared to do as much 'homework' as Berenson did can expect some commensurate rewards!

Fortunately it is not difficult to obtain access to a wide range of works of art under the best possible conditions for viewing, though obviously the concentration of collections open to public view is much greater in the capital cities of relatively civilized countries than, say, in the Great Gromboolian Outback. In the London area, for instance, besides the superb collections at the National Gallery, the National Portrait Gallery, the Tate Gallery, the Wallace Collection, the Victoria and Albert Museum and the British Museum, there are less well-known but quite admirable displays of pictures at the Dulwich Gallery; at Ken Wood House on Hampstead Heath; at the Courtauld Collection in Woburn Square, where some magnificent works by the French Impressionists and Post-Impressionists are on view; at Captain Coram's Foundling Hospital, 40 Brunswick Square; and at several other galleries such as Leighton House, the Wellington Museum at Apsley House, Hyde Park Corner, and the Bethnal Green Museum which have a smaller range of exhibits or a more limited appeal. At Sir John Soane's Museum in Lincoln's Inn Fields, already mentioned in Chapter 7, the casual visitor can spend an afternoon studying the original paintings Hogarth made for his famous series *The Rake's Progress*—and they can be enjoyed, here, in the intimate conditions of the great architect's home. Modern paintings, by all the most significant contemporary artists, can be seen in a score of dealers' galleries. At most of these, visitors are welcome without charge, even if they have no immediate intention of becoming customers. With so many opportunities for looking at pictures, there is no reason why anyone within reach of one of the great art centres should not develop a nice artistic discrimination within a relatively short period of time.

A well-known dealer was once asked if he could give the readers of a popular magazine some helpful advice about buying pictures. The advice he gave (or the gist of it) was something like this:

'Don't worry too much about the possible market value of any picture you are offered. You—and only you—know how much you like that picture, and how much lasting pleasure it is likely to give you as a picture, not as an investment. If it seems to be in first class condition, and if the price seems to be fair in relation to the personal pleasure it is going to give you, buy it. If you are considering it for any other reason, leave it alone.'

And that brings us right back to where we started in Chapter 1—with the advantages of collecting for pleasure. Perhaps this book will have shown you some of the ways in which it is possible for you to get as much enjoyment from your pictures as the richest tycoon does from his—but without having to spend more than a very small percentage of his probable outlay. If it has done this, it will have fulfilled the author's intentions.

INDEX

Aquatint, 99–100
Auctions, 13–14, 42–3, 138

Baxter prints, 101
Bloom, removal of, 124
Book illustrations, 82, 85

Canvases, re-lining of, 126–7
——, restretching of, 55
——, torn, 125–6
Cleaning and restoring, 122–7
Collecting: drawings, 74–85
——, lithographs, 105–12
——, oil paintings, 53
——, prints, 86–104
——, sporting pictures, 114–21
——, water-colours, 64–7
Collectors, great, 22–4
Cracks in oil paintings, 124–5

Dealers' galleries, 44–8
Drawings, pen and ink, 80–2
Drypoint, 99

Engraving, line, 92–6
——, wood, 90–1
Etching, 96–9
——, soft ground, 98–9

Fakes, 76, 128–37
Forgeries, 76, 128–37
Framing, 34–41

Grounds, 56

Hanging of pictures, 25–8

Impressionism, 20–1
Intaglio printing, 86

Lighting, 25, 28
Line engraving: see Engraving
Linocuts, 91–2
Lithographs, collection of: see
    Collecting
Loops, running, 27

Mezzotint, 100–1
Miniatures, 48–9
Mitre-blocks, 39
Mitre-box, 39
Mounting pictures, 30–4
Movements, modern, 21

Norwich School, 71–2

Oil paintings, collection of: see
    Collecting

Papers, 65–6, 75–6, 103
Passe-partout, 34–8
Pastels, 77–8
Pen and ink drawing: see Draw-
    ings
Pentimenti, 63
Pliers, straining, 55
Post-impressionism, 21
Pre-Raphaelite Brotherhood,
    The, 56, 72

Prints, collection of: *see* Collecting

Prints, screen, 112–13

Racks, picture, 29
Re-lining of canvases: *see* Canvases
Restoring: *see* Cleaning and Restoring
Restretching of canvases: *see* Canvases

Silhouettes, 49–51

Soft ground etchings: *see* Etching
Sporting prints, collection of: *see* Collecting
Surface printing, 87
Stretchers, 54

Varnish, 56–8
Veneer, 40

Water-colours, collection of: *see* Collecting